I GIVE YOU
Glory,
O GOD

***Also by Jerry Bridges
in Large Print:***

I Exalt You, O God, Book One
I Will Follow You, O God, Book Two

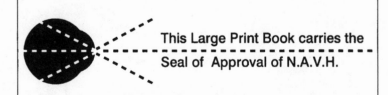

I GIVE YOU *Glory,* O GOD

Honoring His Righteousness
in Your Private Worship

JERRY BRIDGES

Thorndike Press • Waterville, Maine

Published in 2003 by arrangement with WaterBrook Press, a division of Random House, Inc.

Thorndike Press® Large Print Inspirational Series.

The tree indicium is a trademark of Thorndike Press.

The text of this Large Print edition is unabridged.
Other aspects of the book may vary from the original edition.

Set in 16 pt. Plantin by Liana M. Walker.

Printed in the United States on permanent paper.

Library of Congress Cataloging-in-Publication Data

Bridges, Jerry.
    I give you glory, O God : honoring His righteousness in
    your private worship / Jerry Bridges.
        p. cm.
    "This book incorporates content originally included in
    The joy of fearing God" — T.p. verso. Includes
    bibliographical references and index.
    ISBN 0-7862-4950-1 (lg. print : hc : alk. paper)
    1. God — Worship and love. 2. Large type books.
  I. Bridges, Jerry. Joy of fearing God. II. Title.
  BV4817.B673 2003
  248.3—dc21   2002043003

I GIVE YOU
Glory,
O GOD

National Association for Visually Handicapped
------------------------ *serving the partially seeing*

As the Founder/CEO of NAVH, the only national health agency solely devoted to those who, although not totally blind, have an eye disease which could lead to serious visual impairment, I am pleased to recognize Thorndike Press as one of the leading publishers in the large print field.

Founded in 1954 in San Francisco to prepare large print textbooks for partially seeing children, NAVH became the pioneer and standard setting agency in the preparation of large type.

Today, those publishers who meet our standards carry the prestigious "Seal of Approval" indicating high quality large print. We are delighted that Thorndike Press is one of the publishers whose titles meet these standards. We are also pleased to recognize the significant contribution Thorndike Press is making in this important and growing field.

Lorraine H. Marchi, L.H.D.
Founder/CEO
NAVH

CONTENTS

Part III: *I Want to Glorify You, O God . . .*
Living as Your Child

Part IV: *I Want to Glorify You, O God . . .*
Living by Your Wisdom

Part V: *I Want to Glorify You, O God . . .*
And Enjoy You Forever

If there be enough in God to satisfy the angels, then sure there is enough to satisfy us. . . . Fresh joys spring continually from his face; and he is as much to be desired after millions of years by glorified souls as at the first moment. There is a fullness in God that satisfies, and yet so much sweetness, that the soul still desires. God is a delicious good.

— THOMAS WATSON (1620–1686),
"MAN'S CHIEF END" IN
A BODY OF DIVINITY

Introduction

DELIGHTING IN GOD

The *Westminster Shorter Catechism* rightly answers the question, "What is the chief end of man?" by saying, "Man's chief end is to glorify God, and to enjoy him forever." When the writers of the catechism taught us this, they did not say these are humankind's chief *ends,* but our chief *end.* The word is singular. Both glorifying God and enjoying Him together form one aim.

There was a time when I did regard them as two different aims, even assigning different time frames to them. I was expected, so I thought, to glorify God in this life, and then in eternity I would get to enjoy Him.

Perhaps I unconsciously thought of these two parts of our aim in the same way some people think about work and retirement. You *work* for forty or so years, then you get to *enjoy* being retired, but "ne'er the twain shall meet." Don't expect to enjoy your work and avoid all work in your retirement.

The truth is, though, that we cannot glorify God — either by our lives or by worship — unless we are enjoying Him. How could you praise someone whom you don't enjoy? How could you genuinely seek to honor someone by your conduct merely out of a sense of obligation?

As we probe these questions, we can see that glorifying God and enjoying Him are really two sides of the same coin.

John Piper even goes a bit further. He says, "The chief end of man is to glorify God *by* enjoying him forever" (emphasis added).[1] Piper is fond of saying, "God is most glorified in me when I am most satisfied in Him." That is, to the extent that we find our delight in God, we glorify Him.

GAZING UPON GOD — AND WANTING MORE

In Psalm 27:4, David spoke of his delight in God:

> *One thing I ask of the LORD,*
>   *this is what I seek:*
> *that I may dwell in the house of the LORD*
>   *all the days of my life,*
> *to gaze upon the beauty of the LORD*
>   *and to seek him in his temple.*

David asked one thing of the Lord: to enjoy Him. David wanted to *gaze* upon His beauty and *seek* Him in His temple. To gaze is to look intently with wonder or admiration. A young man discovers the girl of his dreams across the aisle at church one Sunday. Before he even begins to initiate a relationship, he seeks inconspicuous opportunities to gaze upon her beauty.

This is what David wanted to do, and he was unabashed about it. He wanted to gaze upon the beauty of God's revealed glory, and he wanted everyone to know it.

David said next in Psalm 27:4 that he wanted to *seek* God. To seek is to search for something of value or something greatly desired. David sought a relationship with God. He wanted to enjoy God and gaze upon His beauty.

Psalm 27:4 is not an isolated text. David wrote in a similar fashion in Psalm 63:1-4:

> *O God, you are my God,*
> *   earnestly I seek you;*
> *my soul thirsts for you,*
> *   my body longs for you,*
> *in a dry and weary land*
> *   where there is no water.*
> *I have seen you in the sanctuary*

and beheld your power and your glory.
Because your love is better than life,
 my lips will glorify you.
I will praise you as long as I live,
 and in your name I will lift up my hands.

If anything, David is even more expressive here than in Psalm 27. He *earnestly* seeks God; his soul *thirsts* for Him, and his body *longs* for Him. Why does he use such intense words? David had beheld God's power and glory and had experienced His love. As a result, he wanted even more to enjoy God and praise Him.

The original publisher of this book is WaterBrook Press. That name is taken from Psalm 42: "As the deer pants for the water brooks, so my soul pants for Thee, O God" (verse 1, NASB). The psalmist continues in verse 2, "My soul thirsts for God, for the living God; when shall I come and appear before God?" Once again we see this intense longing for God. We long for God's blessings; the psalmist longed for God Himself. He wanted to experience the reality of a relationship with God. Like the apostle Paul, he wanted to know Him *fully* — "I want to know Christ," Paul said, "and the power of his resurrection and the fellowship of sharing in his sufferings" (Philippians 3:10).

A similar yearning of God's people is expressed by the prophet in Isaiah 26:8-9:

Yes, LORD, walking in the way of your laws,
  we wait for you;
your name and renown
  are the desire of our hearts.
My soul yearns for you in the night;
  in the morning my spirit longs for you.
When your judgments come upon the earth,
  the people of the world learn righteousness.

God's "name and renown" here speak of His glory; so God's glory was the desire of their hearts. Notice, then, how Isaiah associates a desire for God's glory with a desire for God Himself. He yearned for Him in the night, and as he awakened in the morning, his spirit longed for God.

We cannot long for God's glory to be manifested unless we also long *for Him.*

We cannot glorify God unless we enjoy Him.

Let's be honest, though. Do passages such as Psalm 27:4 describe you? If you're reading this and thinking, *I sure don't desire God as David did,* I suggest you begin to pray over that verse or similar portions of Scripture, asking God to make them a reality in your life.

15

You may need to pray as I sometimes do: "Lord, my sin is more real to me than You are. Help me to know You and desire You as David did."

And remember that I'm setting before you the ideal we should aim for. None of us is there yet, but we should keep pursuing it.

YOUR PRIVATE WORSHIP

I Give You Glory, O God is presented as a companion and guide to your private worship — to help you grow in longing for God and gazing upon Him in delight — and is arranged in the same format as *I Exalt You, O God* and *I Will Follow You, O God.*

As I pointed out in those books and in *The Joy of Fearing God,* both private and corporate worship — that which we do individually and that which we do with other believers — are taught in Scripture, and the vitality and genuineness of corporate worship are to a large degree dependent upon the vitality of our individual private worship.

To grow in glorifying God in our private worship, we would do well to ask ourselves these questions:

1. Have I presented myself and all that I have to God as a living sacrifice, so that my way of life is a life of worship?

2. Do I take time daily to worship God privately and to thank Him for all His blessings to me?

3. Is there some "cherished" sin, some practice I'm unwilling to give up, that hinders my worship?

4. Do I seek to enter wholeheartedly and "in spirit and truth" into worship? Or do I simply go through the motions without really worshiping?

None of us will score perfectly on these questions. That is not their intent. Rather they're designed to help us honestly assess ourselves and pinpoint areas of our lives that need improvement. Only then, and as we take steps to improve, will this book be of benefit to us.

Part I

I Want to Glorify You, O God . . .

IN ALL I DO

~

O worship the King, all glorious above!
O gratefully sing His power and His love!
Our Shield and Defender, the Ancient of days,
Pavilioned in splendour, and girded with praise.
— ROBERT GRANT, 1833

Direct, control, suggest, this day,
All I design, or do, or say
That all my powers, with all their might,
In Thy sole glory may unite.
— THOMAS TEN, 1695

Whate'er I do, things great or small,
Whate'er I speak or frame,
Thy glory may I seek in all,
Do all in Jesus' Name.
— HENRY W. BALDER, 1875

Day 1

HOW WE GLORIFY
GOD

The glory of God is the sum of all His infinite excellence and praiseworthiness set forth in display. To glorify God is first of all to respond properly to this display by ascribing to Him the honor and adoration due Him because of His excellence. We call this *worship*.

Another way we glorify God is by reflecting His glory to those around us in the way we live our daily lives. Jesus said, "Let your light shine before men in such a way that they may see your good works, and *glorify* your Father who is in heaven" (Matthew 5:16, NASB).[2] And R. C. H. Lenski wrote, "We do all things for 'God's glory' when the excellence of God's attributes is made to shine forth by our actions so that men may see it."[3]

What is your aim in life? Is it to be successful or happy or prosperous in whatever you choose to pursue? Is it to be well thought of as a parent, or as a professional person, or even as a Christian? Does your aim terminate on yourself or your family?

What is your true aim?

If we're to glorify God in the way we live, we must make God's glory our primary aim. All other goals in life, both temporal and spiritual, must be secondary. We must seek first His kingdom and His righteousness before everything else. For example, the Christian student should aim at God's glory ahead of academic excellence or popularity or athletic achievement. That doesn't mean he or she should not strive to be a good student or athlete, or be well thought of by other students. But the student should seek those things with the aim of glorifying God, and only in such ways that God is glorified.

When our son was a junior in a Christian high school, his basketball team went to the state tournament for the first time in the school's history. They lost their first game by one point to the team that eventually won the state championship. The sports editor of our local newspaper, who often comes across as rather hard-bitten and cynical, wrote his next editorial about the game. The thrust of his column was about the outstanding sportsmanship of the Christian team. After commenting on several specific instances of the team's conduct during the game, he wrote, "This is how basketball was meant to be played."

Did the boys play hard to win? Absolutely. Were they disappointed to lose by one point? Sure they were. Was God glorified in the way they played? Yes.

When a crusty sports editor recognizes the difference in sportsmanship between believers and unbelievers, God is glorified. To me as a parent, that article was more valuable than if the boys had brought home the state championship trophy.

What is true of the Christian student should also be true of those of us who are adults. All the activities of life should be pursued with the aim of glorifying God. Note the all-encompassing breadth of Paul's words in 1 Corinthians 10:31: "*Whatever* you do, do it *all* for the glory of God." Nothing in life is too ordinary or insignificant to be excluded. Even our eating and drinking are to be done for God's glory. Nothing is so important that we can say it supersedes the pursuit of God's glory.

Are you about to close a lucrative business deal or make a major career decision or launch into some other major endeavor? God's glory should be your first consider-

ation in your business or your career. All of
life is to be lived for the glory of God.

~

*Father, I make the commitment before You, by
Your grace and power, to seek first Your
kingdom and Your righteousness.*

*I praise You for Your righteousness. "Your
righteousness is like the mighty mountains,
your justice like the great deep." "Your righteousness is everlasting and your law is true."
"You love righteousness and hate wickedness."*
Psalms 36:6; 119:142; 45:7

*"Righteousness and justice are the founda-
tion of your throne; love and faithfulness go before you."* Psalm 89:14

*I also praise You for Your kingdom. "Your
kingdom is an everlasting kingdom, and your
dominion endures through all generations."
"You rule over all the kingdoms of the nations.
Power and might are in your hand, and no one
can withstand you." "Your throne, O God, will
last for ever and ever; a scepter of justice will be
the scepter of your kingdom."* Psalm 145:13;
2 Chronicles 20:6; Psalm 45:6

*You are the "true God . . . the living God, the
eternal King." "You, O LORD, reign forever;
your throne endures from generation to generation."* Jeremiah 10:10; Lamentations 5:19

My desire is to commit this day and my life to Your glory. "Blessed be your glorious name, and may it be exalted above all blessing and praise." Nehemiah 9:5

"I will praise you, O Lord my God, with all my heart; I will glorify your name forever." Psalm 86:12

"Now to the King eternal, immortal, invisible, the only God, be honor and glory for ever and ever. Amen." 1 Timothy 1:17

Day 2

SO OTHERS
CAN SEE HIM

In this matter of glorifying God, let's get down to those nitty-gritty details of everyday life.

When you are driving, is your first priority to glorify God or to get where you're going as quickly as possible? When you go shopping, do you treat salespeople in such a way that if they knew you were a Christian, they would see God glorified in you?

My wife and I once stopped at a bakery with what we thought was a "two for the price of one" coupon. It's a small specialty bakery where a salesclerk waits on each customer. My wife selected two loaves of bread and handed the young lady our coupon. "I'm sorry," the clerk said, "but this coupon is good only at the new store we just opened." The coupon didn't state this limitation, but that's what the bakery intended, and they stuck to it (not good customer relations in my opinion, but that's beside the point of the story). My wife said, "Well, just give me one loaf," and she paid for it. As the clerk entered the transaction in her cash register she said to us, "You people are so nice to me."

"What do you mean?" I asked.

"People have been angry at me all day over this coupon deal," she replied, "and you didn't get angry."

Later my wife and I talked about how we could have used that brief conversation as a means of witness, which we had failed to do. But the lesson I learned from that minor shopping event is this: As a Christian I am never "off duty." Even in such an ordinary event as buying a loaf of bread, I have an opportunity to either glorify God or shame Him by the way I conduct myself.

So what should be my aim in such a situation? Should it be to glorify God or to vent my disappointment and displeasure at the bakery because of their promotional mistake? I'm not dealing in trivialities here. Events like these make up most of our existence. Life is largely a mosaic of little things: routine events, everyday duties, and ordinary conversations. How we conduct ourselves in these circumstances determines to a great extent whether we glorify God in our lives.

It's so easy to let a statement such as "Man's chief end is to glorify God" roll off our tongues without really knowing what we're saying. So a couple of years ago I decided to do a Bible study on the subject of glorifying God. I wanted to find out what the Bible says about it. How do we glorify God? I found a number of answers, but what caught my attention was how our actions toward other people determine whether we glorify God or shame Him.

In Titus 2:4-5 Paul gave a list of what older women should train the younger women to do: "to love their husbands and children, to be self-controlled and pure, to be busy at home, to be kind, and to be subject to their husbands, *so that no one will malign the word of God.*" This last phrase is a remarkable statement. There's nothing extraordinary about any of the items on that list. They're all part of the routine of daily living. Yet Paul implied that failure in any of those areas discredits God and His Word, while a life lived as Paul described will glorify God.

A couple of paragraphs later Paul made a

similar statement about slaves: "Teach slaves to be subject to their masters in everything, to try to please them, not to talk back to them, and not to steal from them, but to show that they can be fully trusted, *so that in every way they will make the teaching about God our Savior attractive*" (Titus 2:9-10).

Have you ever considered that the way you fulfill your duties at work or the way you perform your professional services can make the teaching about God attractive? Why isn't the gospel more attractive to unbelievers today? Isn't one primary reason the fact that in the everyday affairs of life, we Christians are no different from the general mass of unbelievers? Sure, we may not get drunk or commit adultery, but do we buy and sell, work at our jobs, play at our various sports, or drive on the road in such a way as to glorify God and make His gospel attractive to those who see us?

Paul asked the religious Jews of his day, "You who brag about the law, do you dishonor God by breaking the law? As it is written: 'God's name is blasphemed among the Gentiles because of you'" (Romans 2:23-24). Isn't this true to some degree today? A person with a Christian fish symbol on his car drives in a discourteous or reckless manner and causes God's name to be ridiculed by unbelievers. I read an article in which the son of a prominent minister was quoted as saying, "If God is like my father, I want nothing to do with Him." The father undoubtedly thought he was glorifying God in the pulpit, but he must have been blaspheming Him in the home.

"Nothing in our conduct," wrote New Testament theologian Simon J. Kistemaker,

should obstruct God's glory from being reflected in us. That is, in everything we do and say, no matter how insignificant, the world should be able to see that we are God's people. Exalting God's glory ought to be our chief purpose in this earthly life.[4]

～

"O Lord, open my lips, and my mouth will declare your praise." Psalm 51:15.

I thank You for Your own commitment to Your glory. "For the earth will be filled with the knowledge of the glory of the LORD, as the waters cover the sea." Habakkuk 2:14

Father, I want to obey Your command to all of us. "Live your lives as strangers here in reverent fear." 1 Peter 1:17

"My soul will rejoice in the LORD and delight in his salvation. My whole being will ex-

claim, 'Who is like you, O LORD?'" "I will give thanks to the LORD because of his righteousness and will sing praise to the name of the LORD Most High." Psalms 35:9-10; 7:17

Day 3

THOSE RECURRING STRUGGLES

For many of us, certain recurring struggles pose a special challenge for us in glorifying God. It may be a tough work environment where there's the temptation to join a crowd of complaining and negative employees. It could be the hassle of a long daily commute to work where you're competing with other drivers for the faster lane. Perhaps it's a difficult home situation because of an unsupportive spouse or children resisting parental authority. One young couple I know has had to deal with a landlord who causes them repeated distress.

Can you think of a recurring situation in your own life where you need to make a special effort to glorify God? For me it's airplane trips. Since a large part of my work and ministry is conference speaking, I make about twenty-five trips a year. Our city has few direct flights to other cities, so I usually have to take two or more connecting flights going and again returning. That means I have about a hundred airplane boardings every year. With that much exposure and the crowded flights of today, there's ample opportunity to think only of myself. I want to board early enough to make sure I get my carry-on luggage into the overhead compartment before the "inconsiderate" people (with the big bags) take up all the space. Or if a flight is canceled, I want to be near the front of the line at the airline service counter to get rebooked. After all, I do have to be at my destination by a certain time. At least that's the way I tend to think.

My first priority, though, is not to arrive at my destination on time or to get my carry-on bag into the overhead compartment. My first priority is that in all of those activities, I will glorify God by my behavior.

Aboard one recent flight, an attendant thanked me for being so nice. Actually I hadn't done anything. What I had *not* done was complain as other passengers around me had because the coffeemaker in the airplane galley wasn't working. This time I was obviously a Christian because I was reading my Bible, so it was a clear opportunity to honor or dishonor God by my behavior.

There's another lesson to be learned from

such incidents. Life is a hassle for most people today. That means abundant opportunities to glorify God in how we treat others or in how we respond to their treatment of us.

I suggest that in active dependence on God you think through your day, asking God for His direction and enablement in each anticipated activity. And if you have a recurring routine where you face the temptation not to glorify God in your behavior, pray over that event beforehand — daily, if it's a daily event — asking God to help you remember that your aim is to glorify Him in that situation. And even for nonrecurring events, if you know of them beforehand, pray about them. Remember that although we are responsible to glorify God in all we do, we are dependent upon the power of the Holy Spirit to work in us and enable us.

~

Thank You for all my prayers You have answered. "When I called, you answered me." And I thank You in advance for the prayers You will answer in the future. Psalm 138:3

Heavenly Father, as I grow — by Your grace and power — in living in dependence on You, let my life bring You glory!
"My soul will boast in the LORD." Psalm 34:2

"I will exalt you, my God the King; I will praise your name for ever and ever. Every day I will praise you and extol your name for ever and ever." Psalm 145:1-2

Day 4

GOD'S GLORY AND MY NEIGHBOR'S WELL-BEING

Paul's exhortation to do *everything* to the glory of God was a response to a specific situation in the Corinthian church — namely, whether it was permissible for believers to eat meat previously offered as a sacrifice to an idol. Some of the Corinthians recognized that an idol was nothing, so they had perfect freedom in their consciences to eat the meat.

Others were still so accustomed to idols that when they ate the meat, they associated it with idolatry, and their weak or overly scrupulous consciences were defiled. They felt guilty as if they had sinned, which indeed they had if they had acted against their consciences. (See Romans 14:22-23.)

Paul agreed with those who felt free to eat the meat, but he wanted them to be considerate of their "weaker" brothers and sisters in Christ. (See 1 Corinthians 8:1-13 and

10:23-33 for Paul's treatment of this problem.) Specifically he said, "Be careful, however, that the exercise of your freedom does not become a stumbling block to the weak" (1 Corinthians 8:9).

Keep this context in mind as we read how Paul concluded his response to this problem:

So whether you eat or drink or whatever you do, do it all for the glory of God. Do not cause anyone to stumble, whether Jews, Greeks or the church of God — even as I try to please everybody in every way. For I am not seeking my own good but the good of many, so that they may be saved. (1 Corinthians 10:31-33)

Paul here set forth two broad principles by which we may gauge our conduct and activities: the glory of God and the well-being, especially the spiritual well-being, of our neighbor. "This is the fundamental principle of practical godliness," wrote Matthew Henry, in commenting on this scripture. "The great end of all practical religion must direct us where particular and express rules are wanting. Nothing must be done against the glory of God and the good of our neighbors."[5]

Charles Hodge wrote in a similar manner: "The first great principle of Christian conduct is to promote the glory of God; the second is to avoid giving offense, or causing men to sin. In other words, love to God and love to men should govern all our conduct."[6] The truth to especially note here is that the glory of God is closely linked with the well-being of our neighbor. We glorify God when we seek our neighbor's well-being.

Who is my neighbor? In the broadest sense it is anyone we come in contact with and whom we have opportunity to treat as we would like to be treated. Paul, though, was referring specifically to a weaker brother or sister who might be tempted to sin because of our exercise of freedom. What's in view here is not a critical, legalistic Christian whose list of don'ts we might have violated, but rather someone who might himself sin because of our example.

A friend of mine had a fairly serious alcohol problem before he became a Christian. Fortunately the Lord enabled him to overcome it, but as you may know, such people are always one drink away from slipping back into their problem. Once while he was on a business trip with some fellow believers, his friends ordered a beer or a glass of wine with their meal. As I understand the Scriptures regarding the use of alcohol, this was within the bounds of their freedom in Christ. However, they did this in full knowledge of the fact that my friend had an alcohol problem. So what happened? He ordered a beer also. He later told me he had a serious struggle not to return to his old ways. His friends failed to glorify God in that situation because they were not sensitive to his weakness.

But should another person's weak conscience or sin problem deprive me of the enjoyment of my freedom in Christ? To answer that question, we need only go back to our aim in life. Is my aim to glorify God or to exercise my freedom?

Glorifying God will often cost us something. It may cost us our freedom in Christ in some situations. It may cost us time or inconvenience or not finding enough space in the overhead bin of a plane for our carry-on bag. It might even cost us a lucrative business deal or an opportunity for career advancement. But Jesus said, "Whoever loses his life for me will save it" (Luke 9:24).

We don't lose our lives all at once, however. We lose them over a lifetime, in individual decisions as we choose whether to glorify God or to satisfy our own desires.

Listen again to Jesus: "Truly, truly, I say to you, unless a grain of wheat falls into the earth and dies, it remains by itself alone; but if it dies, it bears much fruit" (John 12:24, NASB). Jesus later said that we glorify God by bearing "much fruit" (John 15:8). But in John 12, He says we bear "much fruit" by falling into the ground and dying — by losing our lives. If we want to glorify God by bearing fruit we must realize it will often cost us something in one way or other. For this we were created: to glorify God by bearing much fruit, which means we will often have to fall into the earth and die.

∼

Jesus, Lord and Savior, I praise You for Your example for us in dying, that You might live and bear fruit. You "died for all," that we all should no longer live for ourselves but for You. 2 Corinthians 5:15

You are the "King of glory," and I give You praise. You are "the LORD strong and mighty, the LORD mighty in battle," and I give You praise. You are "the LORD Almighty," and I praise You. Psalm 24:8,10

"To the only God our Savior be glory, majesty, power and authority, through Jesus Christ

our Lord, before all ages, now and forever more! Amen." Jude 1:25

"Amen! Praise and glory and wisdom and thanks and honor and power and strength be to our God for ever and ever. Amen!" Revelation 7:12

Day 5

ONLY BY DEPENDING
ON CHRIST

This leads us to another essential aspect of glorifying God in our lives: dependence on Christ. It isn't just good conduct or impeccable character that glorifies God. We all know unbelievers who are morally decent, upright, and generous. Sometimes they put us Christians to shame with their superior behavior. Obviously, though, they do not glorify God. If anything they may, even unintentionally, glorify themselves or their reputations. Others praise them for being gracious or generous or kind. Believers should also desire to be known as gracious, generous, and kind, but we should want the praise or glory directed to God and not to us.

How can we exhibit Christian character and conduct that bring glory to God instead of ourselves? It cannot be done unless we're first depending on Christ. Let me show you why.

Jesus said, "If a man remains in me and I in him, he will bear much fruit" (John 15:5). To *remain* in Christ is what we commonly call *abiding* in Christ. How do we abide? By relying or depending on Him for both our righteousness and our spiritual strength. (See Philippians 3:9 and 4:13.)

The unbeliever who is gracious and generous and kind relies on himself, perhaps influenced by his own moral upbringing, to exhibit those qualities. Sometimes we as Christians do the same, but in this self-reliance we do not bring glory to God. We can bring God glory — what Jesus called bearing fruit — only when we rely on Him for the enabling power to do so.

Paul taught this principle when he prayed that the believers in Philippi would be "filled with the fruit of righteousness that comes through Jesus Christ — to the glory and praise of God" (Philippians 1:11). The only fruit of character that brings glory and praise to God is that which comes through Jesus Christ as we look to Him to work in our lives and enable us to glorify Him.

Peter taught the same principle:

If anyone speaks, he should do it as one speaking the very words of God. If anyone serves, he should do it with the strength God provides, so that in all things God may be praised through Jesus Christ. To him be the glory and the power for ever and ever. Amen. (1 Peter 4:11)

Note what Peter said. If anyone serves, *he should do it with the strength God provides* so that God — not the person, but God — will be praised or glorified. God is glorified not just by gracious and kind behavior, but by behavior that results from a reliance upon Christ.

God is not glorified by self-generated righteousness or human willpower. He is glorified only when we make it our aim both to glorify Him and to depend on Christ through His Spirit to enable us to do so. It is God who must bless our intentions and our efforts to glorify Him, and He blesses when we rely on Christ, not ourselves.

We must not only make it our aim to glorify God; we should also aim *not* to seek glory or praise for ourselves. In Isaiah 42:8, God says, "I am the LORD; that is my name! I will not give my glory to another or my praise to idols." God is jealous for His glory, and He will not share it with us. This speaks not only to our actions but to our motives, which lie totally open before God.

Our problem is that too often we desire —

very subtly and perhaps even uncon-sciously — to share in God's glory. As one of my pastor friends said about his sermons, "I want people to leave the service saying, 'Isn't God great!' but in my heart I hope they also say, 'Isn't Bill great!' " All of us, if we're honest, can identify with my friend Bill. We all want to look good to others, and we all enjoy being commended for our Christian character and good behavior.

What should we do, then, when we are commended; when, for example, someone compliments us for being particularly con-siderate or helpful? Certainly we shouldn't respond with a self-disparaging remark such as, "Oh, it wasn't me. It was the Lord." Such a statement only draws atten-tion to us. Rather we should simply say "Thank you" to the other person, and in our hearts say "Thank you" to God. God, who knows our hearts and sees our desires to glorify Him, will then use our efforts as He sees fit.

❧

In full dependence on You, Lord God, I wor-ship You as my all in all. 1 Corinthians 15:28

I gladly acknowledge my total dependence on You. "In you I trust, O my God" "I trust in your unfailing love; my heart rejoices in your salvation." "I trust in your word." Psalms 25:2; 13:5; 119:42

"You are my Lord; apart from you I have no good thing." I have nothing that I did not receive from You. Psalm 16:2; 1 Corinthians 4:7

I read Your words in the Psalms: "Not to us, O LORD, not to us but to your name be the glory, because of your love and faithfulness." Not to me, O Lord, not to me, but to Your name be the glory. Psalm 115:1

"Glory to God in the highest." "Be exalted, O God, above the heavens, and let your glory be over all the earth." Luke 2:14; Psalm 108:5

Day 6

THE STEWARDSHIP
OF PAIN

Jesus said we're to let our light shine before
men that they may glorify our Father in
heaven. How we behave before other people
is the way we let our light shine. There are
also other ways, and one of the most prominent is by trusting God in our times of adversity.

In an earlier book, *Trusting God*, I wrote,
"It often seems more difficult to trust God
than to obey Him. The moral will of God
given to us in the Bible is rational and rea-
sonable. The circumstances in which we
trust God often appear irrational and inex-
plicable."[7] I wrote those words more than a
decade ago, and I still believe them today.

The thrust of *Trusting God* is probably
best summed up in the statement that God
is infinite in His sovereignty, wisdom, and
love. Because of that, we can be sure that
whatever adversity we may encounter, God

is causing it to work out for our good. With that in mind, I have believed and taught for many years that we are to "give thanks in all circumstances" (1 Thessalonians 5:18), even the difficult ones. We glorify God, then, when we trust Him even when we don't understand what He is doing through the difficult circumstances we encounter. We glorify God when we can say with Job, "Though he slay me, yet will I trust in him" (Job 13:15, KJV).

When we encounter deep heartache or adversity, we may want to deny that God had anything to do with it. This is a common response today and seems to protect God's character, but it does so at the cost of His sovereignty. Another response is to get angry at God, which, of course, means we question both His love and His justice. Or we may simply try to endure the pain, heroically perhaps, but not in a way that honors God. Or we can trust Him because we believe that He is sovereign, wise, and loving.

Several years ago I came across another option that builds upon the foundation of trusting God. This option is called the "stewardship of pain," and I'm indebted to the pastor of my long-ago college days for this concept.[8]

We usually think of Christian steward-ship in terms of money. Some churches have "stewardship campaigns," during which they seek to get their membership to pledge toward the annual church budget. The concept of stewardship was then broadened to include our time and talents — or as one slogan puts it, "Be a good steward of your time, talents, and treasure." The idea behind these concepts is that whatever resources God has given us, He has entrusted them to us as stewards to use for His glory.

Now apply that idea to pain, either physical or emotional. If we believe God is sovereignly in control of all circumstances of our lives, then our pain is something He has given to us just as much as our time or talents or treasure. He has entrusted the pain to us, as stewards, to be used for His glory.

How can we be good stewards of the pain God gives us? One way I've already mentioned is to trust Him even though we don't understand the purpose of the pain. Another way is to ask for and experience the sufficiency of His sustaining grace, as Paul did with his thorn in the flesh, to the extent that we can actually rejoice in our weaknesses so that Christ's power may rest on us (2 Corinthians 12:7-10). We can then, as God gives opportunity, testify to the sufficiency of His sustaining grace. In doing so, however, we want to seek the glory of His grace, not the glory of our ability to endure.

We can also ask God to bring to our attention any opportunities of ministry that our pain may open up. I think immediately of the international ministry that quadriplegic Joni Eareckson Tada has with disabled people and their relatives. I think also of a friend, a woman whose husband divorced her many years ago. Though she went through heartbreaking years as a single parent, today she has a fruitful ministry among other divorced women. She became a steward of her pain.

In one of His post-Resurrection appearances to the disciples, Jesus said to Peter,

"I tell you the truth, when you were younger you dressed yourself and went where you wanted; but when you are old you will stretch out your hands, and someone else will dress you and lead you where you do not want to go." Jesus said this to indicate the kind of death by which Peter would glorify God. Then he said to him, "Follow me!" (John 21:18-19)

Apparently Peter died as a martyr. Tradition tells us he was crucified.[9] Whether that is true or not, Jesus said that by his martyrdom Peter would glorify God. In his pain he would bring glory to God. God wants us to do the same thing with whatever pain He has given us.

~

Heavenly Father, as I grow — by Your grace and power — in living steadfastly and enduring all trials with patience and prayer, let my life bring You glory!

"In your name I will hope, for your name is good." Even in pain I will say, "The Lord is good." Psalm 52:9; 1 Peter 2:3

I trust in You, O Lord. "Into your hands I commit my spirit." Psalm 31:5

Thank You that even in the worst suffering I can say, "In faithfulness you have afflicted me." Psalm 119:75

Thank You that even when my trials bring grief, I can know that You designed them to prove the genuineness of faith, and to cause my faith in the end to result in "praise, glory and honor when Jesus Christ is revealed." 1 Peter 1:6-7

"Praise be to the Lord, to God our Savior, who daily bears our burdens." Psalm 68:19

Day 7

TRUSTING IN HIS PROMISES

Closely akin to trusting God in our pain is trusting Him to fulfill His promises, even when we can't imagine how He can fulfill them. We all know the story of how God promised a son to Abraham, a promise He did not fulfill for twenty-five years. Although Abraham struggled with doubt, he ultimately believed God. (See Genesis 15:2; 16:1-4; 17:17-18.) Paul said of him,

Against all hope, Abraham in hope believed and so became the father of many nations, just as it had been said to him, "So shall your offspring be." Without weakening in his faith, he faced the fact that his body was as good as dead — since he was about a hundred years old — and that Sarah's womb was also dead. Yet he did not waver through unbelief regarding the promise of God, but was strengthened in his faith and gave glory to God, being fully persuaded that God had power to do what he had promised. (Romans 4:18-21)

By his faith Abraham gave glory to God. He ascribed to God the sovereign power to do whatever He purposed and to fulfill all the promises He had made. In that way he gave glory to God.

Today you and I have the same privilege to glorify God by believing His promises. In 2 Corinthians 1:20, Paul wrote,

For no matter how many promises God has made, they are "Yes" in Christ. And so through him the "Amen" is spoken by us to the glory of God.

Every promise God has made is "Yes" in Christ. They will all be fulfilled in Him and through Him. So what is our response to be? It is to say "Amen" to the glory of God. The word *amen* means "it is true." When we say "Amen" to God's promises, we are saying we believe they will be fulfilled, and in that we glorify God.

It isn't easy to believe His promises that are so long outstanding. After two thousand years we're still awaiting Christ's return. Even in the first century, scoffers were ridiculing that promise (2 Peter 3:1-4).

A promise that has been outstanding for some four thousand years is God's word to Abraham in Genesis 22:18, "And through your offspring all nations on earth will be blessed, because you have obeyed me." I understand that promise to mean that from every nation a significant number of people (as opposed to a token few) will be brought into Christ's kingdom. Yet in the world today, we see huge groups of people — Muslims, Hindus, and Buddhists being the largest — who seem almost impervious to the gospel. Will we believe God's promise to Abraham despite these long centuries of delay? Will we continue to plead that promise before Him even if we do not see it fulfilled in our lifetimes? Will we say, "Amen, it is true" and so bring glory to God by believing His promise?

~

"I will be glad and rejoice in your love. . . . I trust in you, O LORD; I say, 'You are my God.' My times are in your hands." Therefore I can say, "In God whose word I praise, in God I trust; I will not be afraid." Psalms 31:7,14-15; 56:4

"You have assigned me my portion and my cup; you have made my lot secure." Psalm 16:5

In my heart I can say with sincerity, "Praise the LORD, for the LORD is good." Psalm 135:3

"Just and true are your ways, King of the ages." Revelation 15:3

"I will say of the LORD, 'He is my refuge and my fortress, my God, in whom I trust.'" Psalm 91:2

I confess this truth about You: "The LORD is good to those whose hope is in him, to the one who seeks him; it is good to wait quietly for the salvation of the LORD." Lamentations 3:25-26

"I will always have hope; I will praise you more and more." Psalm 71:14

With joy I proclaim it: "The LORD is faithful to all his promises and loving toward all he has made." "The LORD is good and his love endures forever; his faithfulness continues through all generations." Psalms 145:13; 100:5

With Your Son, Jesus, I say, "Father, glorify your name!" John 12:28

We glorify God by working out our own salvation. God has twisted together his glory and our good. . . . While we are endeavoring our salvation, we are honoring God. . . . While I am hearing and praying, I am glorifying God; while I am furthering my own glory in heaven, I am increasing God's glory.

We glorify God, by being contented in that state in which Providence has placed us. We give God the glory of his wisdom, when we rest satisfied with what he carves out to us. . . . A good Christian argues thus: It is God that has put me in this condition; he could have raised me higher, if he pleased, but that might have been a snare to me: he has done it in wisdom and love; therefore I will sit down satisfied with my condition. . . . Here, says God, is one after mine own heart; let me do what I will with him, I hear no murmuring, he is content.

As the silkworm, when she weaves her curious work, hides herself under the silk, and is not seen; so when we have done anything praiseworthy, we must hide ourselves under the veil of humility, and transfer the glory of all we have done to God.

— THOMAS WATSON,
"MAN'S CHIEF END" IN
A BODY OF DIVINITY

Part II

I Want to Glorify You, O God . . .

LIVING IN

REVERENTIAL AWE

~

O tell of His might! O sing of His grace!
Whose robe is the light, whose canopy space.
His chariots of wrath the deep thunderclouds form,
And dark is His path on the wings of the storm.
— ROBERT GRANT, 1833

Give me a true regard,
A single, steady aim,
Unmoved by threatening or reward,
To Thee and Thy great Name;
A jealous, just concern
For Thine immortal praise;
A pure desire that all may learn
And glorify Thy grace.
— CHARLES WESLEY, 1742

Day 8

THE JOY OF
FEARING GOD

In this book's introduction we looked at David's delight in God as expressed in the Psalms, a delight in God that led him to earnestly seek and pursue the Lord. Listen again to David's unabashed expression of his desire to gaze upon the beauty of God's revealed glory.

One thing I ask of the LORD,
   this is what I seek:
that I may dwell in the house of the LORD
   all the days of my life,
to gaze upon the beauty of the LORD
   and to seek him in his temple. (Psalm 27:4)

O God, you are my God,
   earnestly I seek you;
my soul thirsts for you,
   my body longs for you,
in a dry and weary land

where there is no water.
I have seen you in the sanctuary
and beheld your power and your glory.
Because your love is better than life,
my lips will glorify you.
I will praise you as long as I live,
and in your name I will lift up my hands.
(Psalm 63:1-4)

We might not otherwise think of it this way, but these phrases from David's psalms are really a description of what is known in Scripture as *the fear of the Lord,* which Sinclair Ferguson describes as "that indefinable mixture of reverence, fear, pleasure, joy, and awe which fills our hearts when we realize who God is and what he has done for us."[10] That is the one thing David wanted. He yearned to experience more fully and consistently the "reverence, fear, pleasure, joy, and awe" that filled his heart when he realized who God is and what He had done for him. He wanted to enjoy the fear of God in the fullest sense of that term.

The underlying principle here is that we grow in the fear of the Lord — in following Him and living rightly before Him in profound, reverential awe — by gazing upon the beauty of His attributes and by seeking an ever-deepening relationship with Him.

To enjoy God is to enjoy the fear of God. And to fear God is by definition to aim for His glory. If we're to be God-fearing people, then the fulfilling and life-stretching truth is that we must make it our aim to glorify Him in all that we are and in all that we do. We cannot truly fear God without seeking His glory.

John Murray described the fear of God as consisting of "awe, reverence, honor, and worship,"[11] and with that perspective in mind, we see that by definition the fear of God focuses on God's glory. *The person who fears God seeks to live all of life to the glory of God.* "Do it all for the glory of God," Paul aptly stated — "whether you eat or drink or whatever you do" (1 Corinthians 10:31).

This connection of the fear of God with the glory of God is brought out clearly in the song of Moses and the Lamb, as the victorious saints sing,

> *Who will not fear you, O Lord,*
> *and bring glory to your name?*
> *For you alone are holy.* (*Revelation 15:4*)

We fear the Lord, or reverence Him, by bringing glory to His name, which involves first of all a *response* to Him and second a *reflection* of Him to others.

We observe this same connection of the fear of God and the glory of God earlier in Revelation, where an angel calls out "in a loud voice" this command from heaven to earth: *"Fear God and give him glory, because the hour of his judgment has come"* (14:7).

The fear of God, the glorifying of God, and the enjoyment of God are so closely intertwined that we cannot separate them. That's why we can say that *there is joy in fearing God* and be both theologically and experientially correct.

~

Dear Father, by Your grace and power let me grow both in delighting in You and in fearing You — and let it all be for Your glory.

"I will be glad and rejoice in you." "My soul will rejoice in the LORD and delight in his salvation." Psalms 9:2; 35:9

"You have made known to me the path of life; you will fill me with joy in your presence, with eternal pleasures at your right hand." Psalm 16:11

"I will bow down . . . and will praise your name for your love and your faithfulness." And before You, I echo David's praise: "Because your love is better than life, my lips will glorify you. I will praise you as long as I live, and in your name I will life up my hands. My soul will

be satisfied as with the richest of foods; with singing lips my mouth will praise you." Psalms 138:2; 63:3-5

"Be exalted, O God, above the heavens; let your glory be over all the earth." Psalm 57:5

Day 9

STORED-UP GOODNESS

Let me give you a reason from my own experience why there is joy in fearing God.
Psalm 31:19 reads,

> *How great is your goodness,*
> *which you have stored up for those*
> *who fear you,*
> *which you bestow in the sight of men*
> *on those who take refuge in you.*

God is pictured here like a wealthy person who establishes trust funds for his children to be used after they reach maturity. The money is on hand; it has been set aside — but it isn't available to the children until they reach the prescribed age.

That is what God does for those who fear Him. He sets aside or stores up goodness for His children, to be given at appropriate times in the future. What this goodness is, and when it will be bestowed, is unique to each individual according to God's plan and purpose for that person.

I came across Psalm 31:19 during one of the more difficult periods of my life. I desperately needed encouragement at the time, and God gave it to me through that passage. What caught my attention was the thought that God *stores up* goodness, which He bestows at some time in the future. Even though life may seem dark today, God is still storing up goodness for us.

As I prayed over Psalm 31:19 during those discouraging days, God gave me hope that at some point in the future He would once again bestow His goodness, the goodness that He was then storing up for me. That's exactly what happened. In due time God opened up ministry opportunities far beyond anything I had ever imagined. Ironically the very circumstances that brought about those discouraging days were used by God to both equip me and set me free for the ministry He had stored up to bestow in His good time.

Notice, though, that God stores up His goodness not for everyone, but for *those who fear Him.* How are we to understand this condition? Why did I think I qualified and had a right to gather confidence from that scripture? This verse is an example of parallelism; that is, where a single idea is stated again in another form. In this case, fearing God and taking refuge in Him are the parallel thoughts. Taking refuge in God is one expression or outworking of fearing Him.

Though my circumstances leading to that discouraging period occurred several years ago, I still remember how the Holy Spirit enabled me to respond. While kneeling at our living room couch early one morning, the words of Job 1:21 came to mind: "The LORD gave and the LORD has taken away; may the name of the LORD be praised." As I prayed over that verse I was able to trust in the sovereignty of God, to believe He was in control of my future, and to submit myself to whatever He was doing. To use the words of 1 Peter 5:6-7, I humbled myself under His mighty hand and trusted Him for the outcome. This is what it meant for me to fear the Lord in that situation. The *joy* of fearing Him did not come immediately, but it certainly did in His good time.

The assurance of future good, however, is not limited just to the difficult periods of life. The Holy Spirit no doubt brought Psalm 31:19 to my attention at that particular time to encourage me and give me hope. The wonderful truth, though, is that

God is always storing up good for those who take refuge in Him, and He bestows it at the proper time. That's why there's joy in fearing God.

~

Father, I am grateful for all the goodness You've stored up for me, ready to be given at the proper time as I take refuge in You. Psalm 31:19

"O LORD, you are my God; I will exalt you and praise your name, for in perfect faithfulness you have done marvelous things, things planned long ago." Isaiah 25:1

"Because you are my help, I sing in the shadow of your wings. My soul clings to you; your right hand upholds me." "For you have delivered me from death and my feet from stumbling, that I may walk before God in the light of life." "You are my God, and I will give you thanks; you are my God and I will exalt you." Psalms 63:7-8; 56:13; 118:28

"Praise be to the LORD, for he showed his wonderful love to me." "Surely God is my help; the Lord is the one who sustains me." "I sought the LORD, and he answered me; he delivered me from all my fears." Psalms 31:21; 54:4; 34:4

Day 10

AWESOME INDEED

What is awe? Like many words in our language, it has several related definitions. My dictionary defines *awe* as:

- an emotion in which dread, veneration, and wonder are variously mingled
- submissive and admiring fear inspired by authority
- a fearful reverence inspired by deity

You can easily see that, depending on the situation and the object of awe, it could include the emotions of fear (or dread), respect (or reverence), admiration, and amazement.

A profound sense of awe toward God is undoubtedly the dominant element in the attitude or set of emotions that the Bible calls "the fear of God." A popular definition of the fear of God is "reverential awe," and I've concluded that this is indeed a good definition.

Why do we say *reverential* awe? It's to indicate that this sense of awe is specifically directed toward God. Imagine yourself driving across one of our central states on a sultry, overcast day. Suddenly you catch sight of a violent tornado spinning across the plains toward you, lifting houses and barns in the air and leaving wholesale destruction in its path. Immediately you feel a gripping sense of awe that includes not only fear for your own safety but also amazement at the storm's overwhelming power. Obviously you're experiencing awe in a very real sense. But it is not reverential awe.

Finally the tornado passes, leaving you safe. You begin to think of the hand of God behind the tornado. You reflect on the fact that the roaring twister was a visible manifestation of His mighty power. Now your awe is focused not on the tornado, but on God. It has become a reverential awe — a mixture of fear, veneration, wonder, and admiration, all directed toward God Himself.

There are indeed many facets to the fear of God and many outworkings of its presence in a believer's life, so to restrict its meaning only to reverential awe would fail to do justice to the biblical concept. But underneath all of these many facets and outworkings is this profound sense of awe toward God that provides the motivation and driving force for all the other elements that together make up the biblical portrait of fearing God.

∾

My Father in heaven, "Who is like you — majestic in holiness, awesome in glory, working wonders?" Exodus 15:11

In this moment I give praise to You, "O LORD, God of heaven, the great and awesome God, who keeps his covenant of love with those who love him and obey his commands." You are "our God, the great, mighty and awesome God." Nehemiah 1:5; 9:32

Thank You for hearing my praise and my prayers. "You answer us with awesome deeds of righteousness, O God our Savior, the hope of all the ends of the earth." Psalm 65:5

Thank You for all that You have done and are doing and will do. "LORD, I have heard of your fame; I stand in awe of your deeds, O LORD." "How awesome are your deeds! So great is your power that your enemies cringe before you." Habakkuk 3:2; Psalm 66:3

Thank You for Your Word, for all that You have spoken. "My flesh trembles in fear of you; I stand in awe of your laws." Psalm 119:120

By the blood of Your Son, Jesus, I draw near to Your throne; in Your presence I praise You: "You are awesome, O God, in your sanctuary." Psalm 68:35

"I will sing praise to your name, O Most High." And my heart exclaims, "How awesome is the LORD Most High, the great King over all the earth!" Psalms 9:2; 47:2

Day 11

WHEN THERE'S REASON
TO FEAR

One problem we face in using the term awe — even *reverential awe* — is that the true meaning of the word is so little understood in our culture today. Its meaning has been essentially debased through frequent flippant usage. It isn't uncommon, for example, to hear someone speak of the awesome chocolate sundae she enjoyed at an ice-cream shop. Compare such a statement with the true meaning of awe as "an emotion in which dread, veneration, and wonder are variously mingled." The ice-cream sundae was undoubtedly tasty, but it hardly qualified as awesome. Even the popular chorus "Our God Is an Awesome God" is too often sung with the gusto and enthusiasm of a pep rally rather than with the sober realization that God is indeed awesome.

Remember again the dictionary meaning

of *awe* and how all three definitions contain the idea of *dread* or *fear*. We can easily see then that it's appropriate to use the word *awesome* to describe a tornado but not an ice-cream sundae. We should be afraid of a tornado; we should enjoy an ice-cream sundae.

Should we be afraid of God? Let's explore this topic first in light of the general situation we've inherited just by being a part of humankind.

As the "only proper answer" to this question, John Murray wrote:

> *It is the essence of impiety [that is, ungodliness] not to be afraid of God when there is reason to [be] afraid. . . . Scripture throughout prescribes the necessity of this fear of God under all the circumstances in which our sinful situation makes us liable to God's righteous judgment.*[12]

After Adam sinned he was afraid (Genesis 3:10). In fact, in his situation it would have been the height of presumption *not* to be afraid. Likewise, when the apostle Paul was describing the abject depravity to which the human race had fallen, he climaxed his descriptive terms with the statement, "there is no fear of God before their eyes" (Romans

73

3:18). People were neither in awe of God nor afraid of His righteous judgments. They acted as if there were no God, no One to whom they were accountable for their conduct, no One who had the power and authority to bring them into judgment for their sins. They essentially thumbed their noses at God.

This lack of fear toward God, in the sense of being afraid of His judgments, is actually the very root of wickedness. John Calvin wrote,

> *All wickedness flows from a disregard of God.... Since the fear of God is the bridle by which our wickedness is held in check, its removal frees us to indulge in every kind of licentious [that is, without moral restraint] conduct.* [13]

Pharaoh is a classic example. He said to Moses, "Who is the LORD, that I should obey him and let Israel go? I do not know the LORD and I will not let Israel go" (Exodus 5:2). Pharaoh was neither in awe of God nor afraid of His judgments. Even after the Egyptians had suffered through seven of the ten plagues, Moses said to Pharaoh, "But I know that you and your officials still do not fear the LORD God" (Exodus 9:30).

In spite of an overwhelming amount of evidence of God's power as shown by the plagues, Pharaoh still was not convinced of God's ability to bring disaster on his land. He still was not afraid of God, so he persisted in his pride and presumption.

The Bible often links a lack of the fear of God with sinful conduct. (For example, see Deuteronomy 25:17-18; Ecclesiastes 8:13; Jeremiah 5:23-24; Malachi 3:5; and Luke 18:1-5.) In fact, the first use of the expression *the fear of God* makes this association. Genesis 20 gives us the account. The patriarch Abraham had moved into the region of a local king, Abimelech, where, for the second time, Abraham lied about Sarah, his wife, saying she was his sister. As a result Abimelech sent for Sarah to make her one of his wives. Fortunately God supernaturally intervened to keep that from happening.

When Abimelech confronted Abraham about his terrible deceitfulness, he asked,

> *"What was your reason for doing this?"*
> *Abraham replied, "I said to myself, 'There is surely no fear of God in this place, and they will kill me because of my wife.'"*
> *(Genesis 20:10-11)*

Abimelech apparently had more integrity than Abraham expected. But Abraham was correct in linking a presumed absence of the fear of God with a lack of moral integrity. Without the fear of God, sin grows unchecked.

~

Righteous Father, You are a "faithful God who does no wrong, upright and just." Deuteronomy 32:4

"Who will not fear you, O Lord, and bring glory to your name? For you alone are holy." Revelation 15:4

Therefore I join with Your angels in heaven to say, "Holy, holy, holy is the LORD Almighty; the whole earth is full of his glory." Isaiah 6:3

"The LORD is in his holy temple; the LORD is on his heavenly throne." Psalm 11:4

"Praise the LORD, O my soul; all my inmost being, praise his holy name." Psalm 103:1

Lord God, I pray to You and praise You, as Your Holy Son, Jesus, taught us: "Our Father in heaven, hallowed be your name." Matthew 6:9

Thank You for teaching us in Your Word about Your absolute holiness. You tell us this:

"The LORD Almighty is the one you are to regard as holy, he is the one you are to fear, he is the one you are to dread." Isaiah 8:13

"Your ways, O God, are holy." Psalm 77:13

Day 12

CONSUMING FIRE

"There is no fear of God before their eyes" (Romans 3:18). What could be more descriptive of large segments of our own society today? Their denial of any objective moral standards, or even their basing of morality upon society's consensus instead of God's Word, is tantamount to saying, "Who is God that we should obey Him?" Like Pharaoh of old, much of society today is neither in awe of God nor afraid of His righteous judgments.

Can you imagine a new class of military recruits making up their own training rules by consensus — or even denying the necessity for any objective training standards? Such a thought is preposterous. It is too absurd even to think of what might happen, since we know that in the very nature of military training it couldn't happen. Yet this is the situation in our society today — and yes, even in our churches.

"In our churches?" you might ask. "Do you mean even Christians should be afraid of God? Haven't we been delivered from the prospect of God's wrath? Doesn't perfect love drive out fear?"

Think of visiting the lion pit at the zoo. The lions are safely separated from you by a large moat and a high fence, so you don't experience the dread or terror that would overtake you if you encountered a lion in the savannas of Africa. Yet even at the zoo you notice a certain caution, a healthy respect, even a nagging fear of the *potential* danger of the lions that makes you glad you're safely separated from them.

Although we've been delivered from the ultimate wrath of God, we are not guaranteed deliverance from His temporal judgments. Aaron's sons Nadab and Abihu were killed instantly for offering unauthorized fire before the Lord (Leviticus 10:1-2). Uzzah was struck down by the Lord for touching the ark of God (2 Samuel 6:6-7), and Ananias and Sapphira died for lying to the apostles and the Holy Spirit (Acts 5:1-11).

It is vain for us to say such judgments from God happened only in biblical times. We have the advantage of divine commentary on those events. We simply don't know today the extent, if any, to which tragic and traumatic events may be the expression of God's judgment against those who do not fear Him. Certainly we should not automatically assume that people, either individuals or groups, who are overtaken by disaster are being punished for their sins. The story of Job refutes that notion. My point is that we should not dismiss the prospect of God's judgment today simply because we don't have clear proof of it. We do know that the apostle Paul warns us to consider *both* the kindness and the severity of God (Romans 11:22, NASB).

It's no longer in good taste in most quarters to speak of the judgment of God or His impending wrath. When we talk about God's "unconditional love" we often mean He simply overlooks or ignores our sinful behavior and would never judge anyone.

But God isn't that way at all. Scripture tells us that "our 'God is a consuming fire' " and cautions us therefore to worship Him "with reverence and awe" (Hebrews 12:28-29).

～

Because You, our God, are "a consuming fire," I come to You "with reverence and awe." Hebrews 12:28-29

I praise You for Your perfect holiness. "Your eyes are too pure to look on evil; you cannot tolerate wrong." "You are not a God who takes pleasure in evil; with you the wicked cannot dwell. The arrogant cannot stand in your presence; you hate all who do wrong. You destroy those who tell lies; bloodthirsty and deceitful men the LORD abhors." Habakkuk 1:13; Psalm 5:4-6

And I praise You for Your promise of holiness for Your people — that one day "they will keep [your] name holy; they will acknowledge the holiness of the Holy One of Jacob, and will stand in awe of the God of Israel." Thank You for Your promise that one day Your people "will bring [you] renown, joy, praise and honor before all nations on earth that hear of all the good things [you] do for [them]; and they will be in awe and will tremble at the abundant prosperity and peace [you] provide for [them]." Isaiah 29:23; Jeremiah 33:9

Day 13

THE SOUL OF GODLINESS

Yes, "Our 'God is a consuming fire' " (Hebrews 12:29) and "a God who expresses his wrath every day" (Psalm 7:11). But He's also good. We must keep both of these truths in mind if we are to understand and practice the fear of God. And, as we'll discover, even God's goodness leads us to a proper fear of Him when we truly understand it.

John Murray offers a compelling reason for why Christians should fear God: "The fear of God is the soul of godliness."[14] That is, the fear of God is the animating and invigorating principle of a godly life. It is the wellspring of all godly desires and aspirations. Do you desire to be a godly person? Then you must understand and grow in the fear of God.

To appreciate that last statement we need to move beyond equating the fear of God only with being afraid of Him. We must not drop that aspect altogether, since even for the Christian it remains an element in the overall concept of fearing God. But it is by no means the dominant element.

What then is that fear of God that is "the soul of godliness"? Note carefully the elements in the following description by John Murray:

The fear of God in which godliness consists is the fear which constrains [compels or powerfully produces] adoration and love. It is the fear which consists in awe, reverence, honor, and worship, and all of these on the highest level of exercise. It is the reflex in our consciousness of the transcendent majesty and holiness of God.[15]

This kind of fear obviously goes beyond simply being afraid of God, for it yields within us such glad responses as adoration, love, honor, and worship. And I would add that these responses are a conscious "reflex" not only to God's "transcendent majesty and holiness," as Murray says, but also to His amazing grace and unfathomable love for us in Christ. We stand in awe not only of God's fiery splendor and absolute purity but also of

His grace and mercy to us.

Respect, admiration, and amazement all intermingle to create the complete sense of awe that is the fear of God, and something less will result if any of those attitudes are lacking. In our understanding of this biblical concept we need to include all three elements:

- respect — which toward God means *reverence* — in recognition of His infinite worth and dignity;
- admiration of His glorious attributes; and
- amazement at His infinite love.

~

Father in heaven, in this moment I tell You from my heart that I respect You with reverence, recognizing Your infinite worth and dignity; I admire Your glorious attributes, which are infinitely great and infinitely good; and I stand amazed at Your infinite love.

"Praise the LORD, O my soul. O LORD my God, you are very great; you are clothed with splendor and majesty." Psalm 104:1

I praise You especially for Your holiness. "You are enthroned as the Holy One." "Your ways, O God, are holy." "Holiness adorns your house for endless days, O LORD." "For the glory of the LORD is great." Psalms 22:3; 77:13; 93:5; 138:5

"I will sing praise to you . . . O Holy One of Israel." Psalm 71:22

Day 14

JESUS DELIGHTED IN FEARING GOD

There are more than 150 references to the fear of God in the Bible.[16] While the majority of these occur in the Old Testament, there are a sufficient number in the New Testament to convince us that fearing God is indeed an attitude of heart we should cultivate today for the glory of God.

Fearing God involves both the most common and the most exalted endeavors in our life. John Murray observes that even "the most practical of mundane duties derive their inspiration and impetus from the fear of God." Then he immediately adds, "The highest reaches of sanctification are realized only in the fear of God."[17] In support of this, Murray cites Colossians 3:22 and 2 Corinthians 7:1. The first passage, addressed to "slaves" or "bondservants," prescribes a level of work that is performed "not with external service . . . but with sincerity of heart, *fearing the Lord"* (NASB). Even the work of slaves is to be done in the fear of God. The same goes for the high pursuit of holiness. In the second passage we're encouraged to "cleanse ourselves from all defilement of flesh and spirit, perfecting holiness *in the fear of God"* (NASB). Note that both of these scriptures occur in the New Testament.

Here are two more: We're given an explicit command to fear God in 1 Peter 2:17: "Show proper respect to everyone: Love the brotherhood of believers, *fear God,* honor the king." And Luke records that after the conversion of Saul the persecutor, the church "was strengthened; and encouraged by the Holy Spirit, it grew in numbers, *living in the fear of the Lord"* (Acts 9:31). God tells us to fear Him, and living that way is the mark of a spiritually healthy body of believers.

One of the most compelling reasons for us to cultivate the fear of God is the example of our Lord Jesus Himself. Consider one of the many messianic prophecies in Isaiah:

A shoot will come up from the stump of Jesse;
from his roots a Branch will bear fruit.
The Spirit of the LORD will rest on him —
  the Spirit of wisdom and of understanding,

the Spirit of counsel and of power,
the Spirit of knowledge and of the fear
of the LORD —
and he will delight in the fear of the LORD.
(11:1-3)

As the Spirit of God rested on the Messiah, one of His endowments would be the fear of the Lord (verse 2). As a result, this prophecy says, "He will delight in the fear of the LORD" (verse 3). This is undoubtedly a reference to Jesus in His humanity. He who was "born of a woman, born under law" (Galatians 4:4) feared God His Father. His heart was completely filled with reverence, awe, honor, adoration, and obedience. And not only was His heart filled, but Scripture adds that He *delighted* in the fear of the Lord. If we would be like the Lord Jesus, we also should delight in fearing God.

～

Father in heaven, I thank You for the example for us of Your Son, Jesus, my Savior, who in the days of His life on earth "offered up prayers and petitions with loud cries and tears to the one who could save him from death, and he was heard because of his reverent submission."Hebrews 5:7

Thank You, Holy Jesus, for submitting to

*Your Father in true reverence. Thank You for becoming a man, and humbling Yourself, and being "obedient to death — even death on a cross!" I know that God has therefore exalted You "to the highest place" and given You "the name that is above every name, that at the name of Jesus every knee should bow, in heaven and on earth and under the earth, and every tongue confess that Jesus Christ is Lord, to the glory of God the Father." I bow before You, and with praise I confess Your name, **Lord Jesus Christ!*** Philippians 2:8-11

Day 15

THE AWE THAT
CHANGES OUR LIVES

To cultivate the fear of God — as God's people should, for His glory — let's analyze it further. Is this fear of God a mix of various emotions, or is it an attitude? Emotions are feelings that come and go, depending on external stimuli, while an attitude is more or less a settled state of mind. Into which category does fearing God belong?

The answer is both. Feelings of awe, reverence, honor, and adoration will definitely be stimulated within us as we have great thoughts about God — as we encounter His majesty, splendor, holiness, and love. Psalm 47 is an example of how thinking great thoughts about God stirs our emotions to fear Him:

Clap your hands, all you nations;
shout to God with cries of joy.
How awesome is the LORD Most High,

the great King over all the earth!
He subdued nations under us,
  peoples under our feet.
He chose our inheritance for us,
  the pride of Jacob, whom he loved.
God has ascended amid shouts of joy,
  the LORD amid the sounding of trumpets.
Sing praises to God, sing praises;
  sing praises to our King, sing praises.
For God is the King of all the earth;
  sing to him a psalm of praise.
God reigns over the nations;
  God is seated on his holy throne.
The nobles of the nations assemble
  as the people of the God of Abraham,
for the kings of the earth belong to God;
  he is greatly exalted.

Notice the expressions here that convey the psalmist's heightened emotions: "Clap your hands" and "shout to God with cries of joy" (verse 1), and "shouts of joy . . . amid the sounding of trumpets" (verse 5). The command to sing praises is given four times in verse 6 and again in verse 7. Obviously the psalmist is excited about God and wants us to share his exuberance.

What is it that awakens such strong emotion in his heart? It is the recognition of God's awesomeness (verse 2) and the confident realization that He is indeed the great King of all the earth (verses 2,7-9). Notice in this passage how great thoughts about God have stimulated emotions that we can rightly call the fear of God. The psalmist is not only deeply stirred in his own heart, but he also wants us to join him in his joyous experience of fearing the Lord.

At the same time, our fear of God must be a settled state of mind — an attitude of awe, reverence, honor, and adoration, a fixed mental outlook that isn't dependent on feelings that come and go. Of course, the right feelings over time will shape our attitude. If we make it a practice to think great thoughts about God, we will develop a sustained attitude of the fear of God.

Whether we think of a complex set of emotions or an attitude, however, the important thing is that this mix is to be *determinative*. The emotions and attitude should determine the way we relate to God — the way we obey Him, trust Him, and worship Him. Properly fearing God is more than just a feeling or attitude — it's a feeling or attitude *that changes our lives.*

Without this proper fear, for example, our view of God may tend toward the servile or slavish type of fear, and our obedience will be somewhat reluctant and driven more by the fear of consequences rather than by a desire to please a loving Father. On the other hand, if our approach to God lacks the proper dimension of awe that has regard to His majesty, splendor, power, and dignity, we'll tend to be overly familiar with God and lacking in reverence toward Him.

So the right fear of God is not just a concept to be entertained in our minds. Rather, it's an invigorating and guiding principle that deeply affects every area of our lives and deter mines the way we live.

∽

Great and mighty God, as I grow — by Your grace and power — in concentrating my mind and my heart on You, let my thoughts and my emotions bring You glory!

"I will praise you, O LORD, with all my heart." Psalm 9:1

"I will sing with my spirit . . . I will also sing with my mind." 1 Corinthians 14:15

"Praise the LORD, O my soul; all my inmost being. Praise his holy name." Psalm 103:1

"May the words of my mouth and the meditation of my heart be pleasing in your sight, O LORD, my Rock and my Redeemer." Psalm 19:14

Day 16

IN GOD'S
VERY PRESENCE

Another dimension of fearing God is the awe of His person, being in awe of God *simply because He is God.* We see this in the lives of several people in Scripture, including Gideon, Job, Isaiah, and Ezekiel (Judges 6:22-23; Job 42:5-6; Isaiah 6:1-5; Ezekiel 1:25-28).

There's one other man in the Old Testament — Jacob — whose encounter with God we want to examine more closely to help us understand what it means to be in awe of God's person.

Jacob was running for his life. He had deceived his father and had stolen from his brother both the birthright and the eldest son's blessing. His brother, Esau, held a grudge against Jacob and purposed to kill him. Jacob was fleeing to his uncle's home in faraway Haran.

The first night of his journey, Jacob had a dream. Notice carefully the five promises

God made to him in this dream, as recorded for us in Genesis 28:12-15:

He had a dream in which he saw a stairway resting on the earth, with its top reaching to heaven, and the angels of God were ascending and descending on it. There above it stood the LORD, and he said: "I am the LORD, the God of your father Abraham and the God of Isaac. I will give you and your descendants the land on which you are lying. Your descendants will be like the dust of the earth, and you will spread out to the west and to the east, to the north and to the south. All peoples on earth will be blessed through you and your offspring. I am with you and will watch over you wherever you go, and I will bring you back to this land. I will not leave you until I have done what I have promised you."

God said nothing in the dream about Jacob's deceitful character or actions. God did not reprimand him or threaten to punish him. Instead He gave Jacob five astounding promises related to possessing the land of Israel, having a multitude of descendants, being a blessing to everyone on the earth, and enjoying God's protective guidance and His continual presence.

What was Jacob's reaction to such a wealth of promised blessings? Did he wake up rejoicing and praising God as we might have expected? Here is Jacob's response:

When Jacob awoke from his sleep, he thought, "Surely the LORD is in this place, and I was not aware of it." He was afraid and said, "How awesome is this place! This is none other than the house of God; this is the gate of heaven." (verses 16-17)

Instead of exaltation, Jacob was afraid. Instead of counting his blessings, he said, "How awesome is this place!" What was it that created such a solemn sense of awe in Jacob and made him afraid? We've already seen that God did not reprimand or threaten him in any way. He only gave him promises. Still, Jacob was awestruck and afraid. Why?

The reason for Jacob's fear was the realization that he had somehow been in the very presence of God. It was not the consciousness of his sin but the consciousness of his creaturehood in the presence of deity that created his sense of awe. In the words of Rudolph Otto, Jacob's response was "the emotion of a creature, submerged and overwhelmed by its own nothingness in contrast to that which is supreme above all creatures."[18]

We can begin to understand something of what Jacob felt when he realized he had been in God's presence. It was the realization that he had been in the very presence of God that caused Jacob to be afraid, as he sensed the infinite difference between the creature and the Creator. Jacob experienced an overwhelming awe of God simply because of who God is — infinitely above the most powerful human beings who have ever lived.

~

"Accept, O LORD, the willing praise of my mouth." Psalm 119:108

"O Sovereign LORD, you are God" "Before the mountains were born or you brought forth the earth and the world, from everlasting to everlasting you are God." 2 Samuel 7:28; Psalm 90:2

And in reverent fear I say, "Tremble, O earth, at the presence of the Lord, at the presence of the God of Jacob." Psalm 114:7

I also praise and thank You that "You are God my Savior." "You are God my stronghold." Psalms 25:5; 43:2

You make me "glad with the joy of your pres-

ence." "You will fill me with joy in your presence, with eternal pleasures at your right hand." Psalms 21:6; 16:11

"Blessed are those who have learned to acclaim you, who walk in the light of your presence, O LORD." Psalm 89:15

Day 17

THE CREATURE AND
THE CREATOR

The familiar story of the apostle Peter in
Luke 5:1-11 is another powerful illustration
of the creature's awe in the Creator's presence.

Jesus was using Peter's boat as a place
from which to teach the people crowding
around Him on the shore. When Jesus fin-
ished, He told Peter to move out into deep
water and let down his nets.

Peter and his partners had been up all
night fishing and had caught absolutely
nothing, so they weren't at all eager to
launch out again. In fact they were already
washing their nets when Jesus got into their
boat. You can almost hear the skepticism
and resignation in Peter's voice: "Master,
we've worked hard all night and haven't
caught anything. But because you say so, I
will let down the nets" (verse 5). In addition
to being tired and discouraged from a fruit-

less night's work, Peter was perhaps a bit peeved that this carpenter-turned-teacher would presume to tell him when and where to fish. He knew the worst time for fishing was when the sun was shining on the water. But perhaps to humor Jesus, Peter did as he was instructed.

You know what happened. They caught such a large number of fish that their nets began to break and their boats began to sink. What was Peter's reaction? Was he elated at such a monumental catch of fish? Did he immediately try to recruit Jesus as a new partner and fishing guide?

Instead of elation there was fear (verse 10). Instead of trying to recruit Jesus, Peter fell at His feet and said, "Go away from me, Lord; I am a sinful man!" (verse 8).

Peter had already seen at least one other miracle, when Jesus healed his mother-in-law (Luke 4:38-39). But this one was different. This revelation of Jesus' power over the fish in the lake spoke to him in a special way, because it was in the field of his own trade. He well knew how humanly impossible it was to catch fish during these daylight hours. That's why he fell down before Jesus. Peter was awestruck to realize that he was in God's very presence.

Note that Jesus said nothing about Peter's

sin. Everything was positive. In their nets Peter could see what must have been the equivalent of what it took days or weeks to catch. He should have been excited and rejoicing — except for one thing: He now saw who Jesus really was.[19]

Peter became acutely and painfully aware of his sinfulness. But what made him fall down before Jesus was not his sin, but Jesus' deity. It was the reaction of the creature to his Creator. It was the profound awe of recognizing the vast difference between himself and the infinite, eternal God.

～

"No one is like you, O LORD; you are great, and your name is mighty in power." "Ah, Sovereign LORD, you have made the heavens and the earth by your great power and outstretched arm. Nothing is too hard for you." Jeremiah 10:6; 32:17

"Praise be to the LORD God . . . Praise be to his glorious name forever; may the whole earth be filled with his glory. Amen and Amen." Psalm 72:18-19

Yes, let Your earth-filling glory be seen and known! "For the earth will be filled with the knowledge of the glory of the LORD, as the waters cover the sea." Yes, "the glory of the LORD fills the whole earth." Habakkuk 2:14; Numbers 14:21

"Your kingdom come, your will be done on earth as it is in heaven." Matthew 6:10

"To our God and Father be glory for ever and ever. Amen." Philippians 4:20

Day 18

CROSSING THE

INFINITE DISTANCE

Again and again we see this phenomenon in Scripture — men awestruck in the presence of God.

John Calvin spoke of "that dread and wonder with which Scripture commonly represents the saints as stricken and overcome whenever they felt the presence of God." Then Calvin concluded, "As a consequence, we must infer that man is never sufficiently touched and affected by the awareness of his lowly state until he has compared himself with God's majesty."[20]

One of the more striking illustrations of this profound awe occurred in the life of the aged apostle John. Revelation 1 recounts John's experience of seeing the ascended, glorified Christ in His infinite majesty, power, authority, omniscience, and holiness (1:12-16). John records his reaction: "When I saw him, I fell at his feet as though dead" (verse 17).

Remember, this is the same John who had lived with Jesus for three years, who was part of His inner circle, and who was even called "the disciple whom Jesus loved" (John 13:23). Yet when he saw Jesus in the unveiled glory of His deity, he was awestruck in the most profound way.

This was not the first time John had fallen down before Jesus. The first occasion is recorded in Matthew 17:1-8 when Jesus took Peter, James, and John up on a high mountain and was transfigured before them. There they heard the voice of God saying, "This is my Son, whom I love; with him I am well pleased. Listen to him!" (verse 5). At this the three disciples fell facedown to the ground, terrified (verse 6). In Revelation 1, though, John's awestruckness was highly intensified. The text says, "I fell at his feet *as though dead*" (verse 17).

Peter had fallen at Jesus' knees (Luke 5:8), and the prophet Ezekiel had fallen facedown before the glory of the Lord (Ezekiel 1:28), but only John fell at His feet as though dead. Why did John experience such a life-draining response to Christ's magnificent glory — a response seemingly more profound than anyone had ever experienced?

John was about to receive the most awesome revelation of God ever granted to man. In a series of vivid and striking visions he was to see pictorial representations of God's sovereign rule over all of history, of the final victory of Jesus Christ, the "KING OF KINGS AND LORD OF LORDS" (Revelation 19:16), and finally, of the ushering in of the new heavens and the new earth. It seems that such grand exaltation of John required this severe humbling to prepare him to receive these revelations. Paul had been given his thorn in the flesh *after* his revelations (2 Corinthians 12:1-9). John was humbled in the dust *before* receiving his. In each instance it was to show both them and us that we are at best only "jars of clay" (2 Corinthians 4:7) in which God is pleased to deposit the excellency of His glory.

In responding to God's presence as he did, John could not have helped himself. Nor could Peter when he fell at Jesus' feet after the miraculous catch of fish; nor could Jacob when he awoke afraid from his encounter with God and said, "How awesome is this place!" They had no choice but to respond in deepest awe. Each of them was afraid because each realized he was (or had been, in Jacob's case) in the very presence of God.

Will we, then, have "no choice" but to fall down in awe before God as did Jacob, Peter, and John? That might happen to us on occasion. There have been a few times in my life when the Holy Spirit gave me such an overwhelming realization of God's glorious splendor that I had no choice. I was simply impelled by a spontaneous reaction. Our normal experience, however, will be to quietly and slowly grow in our apprehension of the infinite majesty of God. As this happens we will choose to bow before Him in worship and adoration.

The difference between God and us, even apart from our sin, is an infinite distance. Even if we succeeded in becoming the most powerful human being in all of history, the difference between us and God would still be infinite. And this is the infinite gap that God the Father crosses when He reveals Himself to us and draws us to Himself through His Son, Jesus, and the Holy Spirit.

The God who revealed Himself to Jacob, Peter, and John is the same omnipotent and holy God today. He has revealed to us in His Word all that we need to know of Him to properly fear Him. Though we may not have the same kind of direct encounter with God as did those men, we can encounter Him in

His Word as the Holy Spirit opens it to our minds and hearts.

~

O Lord, great and awesome God, I acknowledge the infinite distance that separates us from Your infinite perfection and power.

Oh, the depth of the riches of Your wisdom and knowledge. How unsearchable are Your judgments, and Your paths beyond tracing out! Romans 11:33

Who could ever comprehend Your mind? Or who could ever be Your counselor? Romans 11:34

Who has ever given to You, that You should repay him? Romans 11:35

For from You, and through You, and to You are all things. To You be the glory forever! Amen. Romans 11:36

Glory is the sparkling of the Deity. . . . A king is a man without his regal ornaments, when his crown and royal robes are taken away; but God's glory is such an essential part of his being, that he cannot be God without it. God's very life lies in his glory. . . .

His glory is his treasure, all his riches lie here. . . . God's glory is more worth than heaven, and more worth than the salvation of all men's souls. Better kingdoms be thrown down, better men and angels be annihilated, than God should lose one jewel of his crown, one beam of his glory.

Faith brings glory to God; it sets to its seal that God is true. . . . God honors faith, because faith honors him. . . . Faith knows there are no impossibilities with God, and will trust him where it cannot trace him. . . . The higher the lark flies the sweeter it sings: and the higher we fly by the wings of faith, the more we enjoy of God. How is the heart inflamed in prayer and meditation! What joy and peace is there in believing! . . . He that enjoys much of God in this life carries heaven about him.

— THOMAS WATSON, "MAN'S CHIEF END" IN A BODY OF DIVINITY

Part III

I Want to Glorify You, O God . . .

LIVING AS YOUR CHILD

~

Frail children of dust, and feeble as frail,
In Thee do we trust, nor find Thee to fail;
Thy mercies, how tender! how firm to the end!
Our Maker, Defender, Redeemer, and Friend!
— ROBERT GRANT, 1833

Crown Him the Lord of Life,
Who triumphed o'er the grave,
And rose victorious in the strife
For those He came to save
His glories now we sing
Who died and rose on high,
Who died, eternal life to bring
And lives that death may die.
— MATTHEW BRIDNEE, 1861

Day 19

HIS SLAVE OR HIS CHILD?

In the fear of God we respect His righteous judgments, but even that aspect of the fear of God should not be a slavish or servile fear. Sinclair Ferguson has made a helpful distinction between "servile fear" and "filial fear." The word *servile* comes from the Latin *servus*, which means "slave," while *filial* is from *filius*, meaning "son." Ferguson explains servile fear as "the kind of fear which a slave would feel towards a harsh and unyielding master."[21]

Servile fear is illustrated by the third servant in Christ's parable of the talents. The servant said to his master, "I knew that you are a hard man, harvesting where you have not sown and gathering where you have not scattered seed. So I was afraid and went out and hid your talent in the ground" (Matthew 25:24-25).

We believers are apt to fall into a servile

fear if we don't fully understand the grace of God and His acceptance of us through Christ. If we believe we're in a performance relationship with God, then He can seem to be a hard taskmaster whom we can never please. We'll see Him as the divine ogre ready to judge us for even our least failure to live up to His rules. We might never express our fear in such bald terms, but such a feeling lurks deep within the hearts of many Christians.

John Bunyan, in his treatise on the fear of God, points to the devil as the author of this servile fear. Bunyan said the devil uses it to haunt and disturb Christians and to make our lives uncomfortable. But we are heirs of God and His kingdom, and Bunyan reproves us for not resisting this slavish fear as we ought. He says we actually rather cherish and entertain this wrong view and thus weaken the filial fear that we instead ought to strengthen.[22]

In contrast to servile fear, filial fear is the loving fear of a child toward his father. It's what Sinclair Ferguson described as "that indefinable mixture of reverence, fear, pleasure, joy and awe which fills our hearts when we realize who God is and what He has done for us."[23] *This is the only true fear of God.* We create that reverence and fear that Ferguson speaks about when we focus on the holiness and greatness of God, when we exult in the infinite wisdom of God, and most of all when our hearts are filled with pleasure and joy as we gaze upon the breadth and length and height and depth of the love of God revealed to us through Christ Jesus.

~

My loving Father in heaven, as Your chosen child, I praise and honor You.

"You, O LORD, are our Father, our Redeemer from of old is your name." Isaiah 63:16

Thank You, Lord Jesus, that You are not ashamed to be my Brother. Thank You for becoming "a merciful and faithful high priest in service to God." Thank You that You have been "faithful as a son over God's house." Hebrews 2:11,17; 3:6

I praise You, Lord Jesus, as "the Amen, the faithful and true witness, the ruler of God's creation." How right it is that Your name is "Faithful and True." Revelation 3:14; 19:11

Day 20

A HEALTHY RESPECT FOR HIS DISCIPLINE

For a number of months prior to writing my book *The Joy of Fearing God,* I prepared by studying many passages of Scripture as well as reading what other authors have written on the subject. As I answered people's questions about what I was working on, I was quite interested in their responses. Most were encouraging, but some were a bit disturbing. People often said something to this effect: "Make sure you emphasize that to fear God really means to FEAR Him!" I got the impression they wanted me to make people afraid of God.

I suspect that those who responded in this way were acutely concerned about the pervasive lack of reverence and awe of God and the consequent disregard of His moral laws that abound in our Christian circles today. I share their concern, but I question this emphasis on being afraid of God.

In Exodus 20:20 we see Moses telling God's people, *"Do not be afraid.* God has come to test you, so that *the fear of God* will be with you to keep you from sinning." Here Moses draws a contrast between being afraid of God and fearing God. Note that this fear of God was to keep them from sinning. *Simply being afraid of God will lead to distrust and disobedience of Him. But fearing God — in the biblical sense — will keep us from sinning.*

Someone may object and refer to 1 Peter 1:17, which tells us, "Since you call on a Father who judges each man's work impartially, live your lives as strangers here in reverent fear." Isn't the fear of God in this verse meant to be a deterrent to disobedience? The Greek word *phobos,* usually translated as "fear," can mean to be afraid in the normal sense of the word, but it can also mean the reverential awe that we call the fear of God. The *New International Version* translates it as "reverent fear," and this is the way we *should* understand it — as the fear of God in the sense of reverential awe.

Peter, however, is setting before us a particular application of this reverent fear. It is meant to be a motivator for our conduct. This fear is intended to stimulate us to holy living. In the verses immediately preceding this one, Peter calls us to be holy because God is holy. In this context of a challenge to holy living, he then reminds us that God judges impartially, that He has no favorite children whom He will allow to get away with disobedience. God is no indulgent grandfather who overlooks our sin.

The particular aspect of the fear of God that Peter has in mind, then, is a healthy respect for God's fatherly discipline. Such a fear is entirely consistent with our assurance of the Father's love for us and with our desire to please Him because of our love for Him.

~

Loving Father, thank You for Your discipline that guides and guards me.

Thank You that by Your mercy, as well as by Your fatherly discipline, You allow me to share in Your holiness. I "have been made holy through the sacrifice of the body of Jesus Christ once for all." You chose me in Christ "before the creation of the world to be holy and blameless" in Your sight. Hebrews 12:10; 10:10; Ephesians 1:4

"O great and powerful God, whose name is the LORD Almighty, great are your purposes

and mighty are your deeds. Your eyes are open to all the ways of men; you reward everyone according to his conduct and as his deeds deserve."
Jeremiah 32:18-19

Day 21

HE DISCIPLINES THOSE HE LOVES

In a well-ordered family we can easily see how a healthy respect for fatherly discipline is consistent with the assurance of fatherly love. The children have a healthy respect for their father's discipline, but they are not afraid of him. They don't live in dread of either physical or emotional abuse (in fact, they may not even be aware there is such a thing), but they know that willful disobedience will bring punishment.

I grew up in a home where I never questioned my father's love for me. At the same time I never questioned his commitment to discipline me (read that as "spank me") when he felt I needed it. My mother's most fearsome words to me were, "I'm going to tell your father when he gets home."

When I was small — four or five years old — my father led the congregational singing in our small church. While the pastor was preaching, my father sat on the platform facing the congregation. Sometimes when I would get unusually wiggly, I would suddenly "feel" his eyes on me. I would look up and see him staring at me with a stern look, and I would immediately stop my wiggling. The prospect of an after-church spanking was all the deterrent I needed. Yet I never doubted my father's love.

That's a small human illustration of what Peter meant when he said, "Live your lives as strangers here in reverent fear" (1 Peter 1:17). Remember, God disciplines those He loves (Hebrews 12:6). Although the word *discipline* in that passage denotes a wider meaning of overall child training, we know that it includes the "spiritual spankings" we all need from time to time. And while God desires that we obey Him because we love Him rather than because we're afraid of Him, He does resort to the punishment aspect of discipline when necessary. We see this clearly in the case of the Corinthian believers who were blatantly abusing the Lord's Supper (1 Corinthians 11:27-32).

Many Christians seem to disregard the prospect of God's discipline. They apparently don't believe that stubborn and persistent continuance in sin will invoke God's fatherly displeasure. They mistake God's grace for a license to live as they please, on the assumption that God's forgiveness is automatic and unconditional. I recall an acquaintance of mine who, in the midst of leaving his wife for another woman, said, "I know this is wrong, but God will forgive me." Unfortunately pastors hear this kind of statement all too frequently.

These people apparently have no fear of God's discipline. They're strangers to the idea of living their lives in reverent fear.

And what about us? Though our disobedience may not be as crass and obvious as that of the man leaving his wife, we can exhibit this same attitude in a more subtle way. Anytime we sin with the thought lurking in the back of our minds that God will forgive us, we aren't living in the fear of God.

It's true, in a judicial sense, that God has already forgiven us all our sins, past, present, and future. As Paul said in Colossians 2:13, "He forgave us all our sins." Christ fully paid for every one of our sins on the Cross, so God no longer counts them against us (see Romans 4:7-8).

However, though God will never judge true believers for their sin, He will discipline us if we persist in an unrepentant attitude toward sin. Lest this last sentence cause anxiety in the mind of someone who struggles with some persistent sinful habit, let me emphasize that God's discipline occurs because of an unrepentant and irreverent attitude — not because of failures in a sincere struggle with sin. There's a vast difference between the attitude of a person who is struggling to put away some sin and the attitude of one who thinks, "I know it's sin, but God will forgive me."

~

"Great is your love, reaching to the heavens; your faithfulness reaches to the skies." Psalm 57:10

"You, O Lord, are a compassionate and gracious God, slow to anger, abounding in love and faithfulness." Psalm 86:15

Father in heaven, thank You for Your compassionate and gracious discipline. Continue to train me with it. "Teach me to do your will, for you are my God; may your good Spirit lead me on level ground." Psalm 143:10-11

"How priceless is your unfailing love!" Psalm 36:7

With Your Son, Jesus, I say, "Father, glorify your name!" John 12:28

~

We glorify God when we are devoted to his service. . . . The wise men that came to Christ did not only bow the knee to him, but presented him with gold and myrrh (Matthew 2:2). So we must not only bow the knee, give God worship, but bring presents of golden obedience. A good Christian is like the sun, which not only sends forth heat, but goes its circuit round the world. Thus, he who glorifies God, has not only his affections heated with love to God, but he goes his circuit too; he moves vigorously in the sphere of obedience.

We aim at God's glory, when we are content that God's will should take place, though it may cross ours. Lord, I am content to be a loser, if thou be a gainer; to have less health, if I have more grace, and thou more glory.

The thief on the cross had dishonored God in his life, but at his death he brought glory to God by confession of sin. . . . A humble confession exalts God. How is God's free grace magnified in crowning those who deserve to be condemned! . . . Confession glorifies God, because it clears him; it acknowledges that he is holy and righteous, whatever he does.

— THOMAS WATSON,
"MAN'S CHIEF END" IN
A BODY OF DIVINITY

Part IV

I Want to Glorify You, O God . . .

LIVING BY YOUR WISDOM

~

The earth, with its store of wonders untold,
Almighty, Thy power hath founded of old,
Hath 'stablished it fast by a changeless decree,
And round it hath cast, like a mantle, the sea.
— ROBERT GRANT, 1833

He rules the world with truth and grace,
And makes the nations prove
The glories of His righteousness,
And wonders of
His love.
ISAAC WATTS, 1719

Day 22

THE ONLY FOUNDATION FOR RIGHT PERSPECTIVES

Proverbs 1:7 reads in full, "The fear of the LORD is the beginning of knowledge, but fools despise wisdom and discipline." *Knowledge* as used here is more than an accumulation of information. It involves the ability to view that information with the right perspective and to use it for its proper end. Paul, for example, speaks of a knowledge that "puffs up" (1 Corinthians 8:1) as well as a knowledge that "leads to godliness" (Titus 1:1). Only the latter has the right perspective and the proper end in mind.

Two people may possess essentially the same knowledge with regard to a body of facts. One person views this knowledge as a means of acquiring position, power, or possessions and uses it to that end. The other person sees it as a gift from God and as a stewardship to be used to serve Him.

Contrast two physicians, both with approximately the same training and skill. One fears God and earnestly seeks to use his expertise to serve Him by serving people. The other has no fear of God and uses his skill as an abortionist. Both doctors have the same information but not the same knowledge. Only the one who fears God has the right perspective, which leads him to use his information for the proper end.

Solomon said that knowledge begins not in learning a body of information or in acquiring various skills, but in the fear of the Lord. He was saying that the fear of God must be the foundation upon which knowledge is built. It is the fear of the Lord that gives us the right perspective and prompts us to use it for the right end. It is the fear of the Lord that should determine our fundamental outlook on life.

Our main goal in life should be to glorify God. That is the ultimate goal to which all knowledge should be directed. Regardless of how helpful an item or body of knowledge may be to society, if it does not have as its final purpose the glory of God, it remains defective. It is at best partial and to a degree distorted. It is like a structure without a foundation, a plant without a root.

Of course, since our fear of God is always imperfect, our knowledge will always be defective and incomplete — not only factually, but also in its use. But the person who does not fear God doesn't even have the right foundation on which to build. He may be a decent person and generally beneficial to society, but in the end he falls short because he neither knows nor fears God. Let me give you an example.

Several years ago I read *Evolution: A Theory in Crisis* by Michael Denton, an Australian physician who does research in microbiology. In my opinion his book is one of the most brilliant and devastating critiques of the theory of evolution available today. Dr. Denton did his homework well. From a number of perspectives he makes a convincing case that animal life as we see it today, and particularly the human body and brain, must be the product of specific design by an infinitely intelligent designer rather than the result of mere time and chance.

As you read through the book, you keep waiting for Dr. Denton to make a seemingly obvious statement that this intelligent designer must be God. Instead, the book ends with this remarkable sentence: "The 'mystery of mysteries' — the origin of new beings on earth — is still largely as enigmatic as when Darwin set sail on the *Beagle*."[24]

After thoroughly debunking the Darwinian theory of evolution, Dr. Denton throws up his hands. "We don't know," he essentially says. We didn't know before Charles Darwin made his observations about plants and animals on the Galapagos Islands, and we still don't know today.

Why would a brilliant scientist come to such a conclusion? The reason is found in Solomon's words that the fear of the Lord is the beginning of knowledge. Dr. Denton has amassed a formidable amount of information and makes a strong case against evolution, but he is unable to bring his reasoning to a successful conclusion because his knowledge is incomplete. It does not take account of God.

I found Dr. Denton's book highly fascinating. In pursuing his objective to show the fallacy of evolution, he unwittingly gave us a book through which to marvel at the unfathomable wisdom of God in creation. On numerous occasions I found myself pausing to worship as I read. *What a pity*, I thought, *that this man who knows a thousand times more than I about his subject could not use it to glorify God because he did not know or fear the One about whom he was writing.*

～

"O LORD, our Lord, how majestic is your

name in all the earth!" Psalm 8:1

"You are the God who performs miracles; you display your power among the peoples." Psalm 77:14

"Yours, O LORD, is the greatness and the power and the glory and the majesty and the splendor, for everything in heaven and earth is yours. Yours, O LORD, is the kingdom; you are exalted as head over all." 1 Chronicles 29:11

"Ah, Sovereign LORD, you have made the heavens and the earth by your great power and outstretched arm. Nothing is too hard for you." Jeremiah 32:17

"You alone are the LORD. You made the heavens, even the highest heavens, and all their starry host, the earth and all that is on it, the seas and all that is in them. You give life to everything, and the multitudes of heaven worship you." Nehemiah 9:6

You are the God *"who created the heavens and stretched them out, who spread out the earth and all that comes out of it, who gives breath to its people, and life to those who walk on it."* You are the God *"who gives life to everything."* Isaiah 42:5; 1 Timothy 6:13

"You are worthy, our Lord and God, to receive glory and honor and power, for you created

all things, and by your will they were created and have their being." Revelation 4:11

I praise You, Jesus my Savior, that in You "are hidden all the treasures of wisdom and knowledge." Thank You for being **my** wisdom — **my** righteousness, **my** holiness, **my** redemption. Colossians 2:3; 1 Corinthians 1:30

"Praise be to the LORD God . . . who alone does marvelous deeds." Psalm 72:18

Day 23

SOURCES OF WONDER

People who fear God can use their knowledge both to glorify God and to enjoy Him.

One day I was waiting in the examining room of an ear, nose, and throat doctor. On the wall opposite my chair was a drawing of a greatly enlarged cross section of the human ear. As I looked at the tiny bones commonly called the hammer, anvil, and stirrup, I marveled at the perfection of the human ear and the ingenuity of God in designing it. I enjoyed a few moments of worship while waiting there and transformed a routine doctor's appointment into a delightful time of fellowship with God. I know very little about the ear, but I can thoroughly enjoy the knowledge I have because it is built upon the foundation of fearing the One who created it.

My experience should be true of the believer in every field of knowledge. The student of history can enjoy the subject much more if he or she believes that history is not merely a "tale told by an idiot," but rather the outworking of God's sovereign plan and purpose for this world. The Christian astronomer should worship as he observes through his telescope the vast handiwork of God in the heavens. The godly farmer growing crops rejoices in the awareness that his agricultural skill comes ultimately from God, because he reads in the Bible that "God instructs him and teaches him the right way" of planting and harvesting (Isaiah 28:26). Any sphere of knowledge you're engaged in — every aspect of your workaday world — should be a source of wonder and worship to you as a believer and should be used as a means of glorifying God. And it will be if you enjoy the fear of God.

Finally, we must consider the most important knowledge of all. Jesus said, "Now this is eternal life: that they may know you, the only true God, and Jesus Christ, whom you have sent" (John 17:3). In reality this is where true knowledge begins. The person who knows God and fears Him possesses something more valuable than all the combined knowledge of philosophy and science put together. The scientist and the philosopher may discover ways to improve this life. The Christian has found the way to *eternal* life.

That the Christian's knowledge is more valuable than any other kind of knowledge was attested to by Jesus when He said, "What good is it for a man to gain the whole world, yet forfeit his soul? Or what can a man give in exchange for his soul?" (Mark 8:36-37).

◆

I praise You for Your wisdom, Lord God. Your "understanding has no limit," and Your "greatness no one can fathom." You indeed perform "great things beyond our understanding." Psalms 147:5; 145:3; Job 37:5

"Many, O LORD my God, are the wonders you have done." Psalm 40:5

"You make me glad by your deeds, O LORD; I sing for joy at the works of your hands. How great are your works, O LORD, how profound your thoughts!" Psalm 92:4-5

You have indeed made "everything beautiful in its time." Ecclesiastes 3:11

I praise and thank You, Lord Jesus, for giving me eternal life by Your death. With the words proclaimed by voices in heaven, I praise You this day: "Worthy is the Lamb, who was slain, to re-

ceive power and wealth and wisdom and strength and honor and glory and praise!" Revelation 5:12

"May the glory of the LORD endure forever; may the LORD rejoice in his works." Psalm 104:31

Thank You especially for the riches of Your grace in Jesus Christ which You have "lavished on us with all wisdom and understanding." Ephesians 1:7

"To the only wise God be glory forever through Jesus Christ! Amen." Romans 16:27

Day 24

ETHICAL AND
PRACTICAL

Proverbs 9:10 says, "The fear of the LORD is the beginning of wisdom, and knowledge of the Holy One is understanding." Note the close connection between wisdom and knowledge. Since wisdom is knowledge applied to the right end, knowledge realizes its purpose only in conjunction with wisdom.

Wisdom is commonly defined as good judgment or the ability to develop the best course of action in response to a given situation. In the Bible, however, wisdom has a strong ethical content. For example, James 3:17 says, "But the wisdom that comes from heaven is first of all pure; then peace-loving, considerate, submissive, full of mercy and good fruit, impartial and sincere."

The ethical emphasis in wisdom is particularly strong in Proverbs. This doesn't exclude what we might call the practical dimension, such as the wise use of time or money. In fact, the book of Proverbs is filled with instructions for day-to-day living. But this practical wisdom always has an ethical tone to it. Wisdom in Proverbs is more concerned with righteous living than with shrewd judgment. The practical is never divorced from the ethical.

It is with this ethical-practical relationship in mind that we should understand how the fear of the Lord is the beginning of wisdom. Just as the fear of God is the foundation of knowledge, so it's also the foundation of wisdom.

Consider, for example, Proverbs 11:1: "The LORD abhors dishonest scales, but accurate weights are his delight." Society says, "Honesty is the best policy." Why? The world's answer is, "It's good for business." The honest auto repair shop gets a good reputation and presumably more cars to repair. Biblical wisdom, however, recognizes that God — even more than the customer — is concerned about honesty. Biblical wisdom always factors God into the equation. Society might cut corners when it isn't apt to hurt business, but the person who fears the Lord strives to be honest all the time. He's more concerned about pleasing God than about what's good for business.

The fact is, honesty *is* the best policy. That's practical wisdom. That's what the world says (though too often it doesn't practice it). But this kind of wisdom has the wrong foundation. It is essentially self-serving. It leads us in the wrong direction and ultimately ends in futility and frustration. By contrast, wisdom based on the fear of God recognizes the supremacy of God over every area of life and realizes that it is God who sends poverty and wealth; He is the One who humbles and exalts (1 Samuel 2:7).

In this, wisdom rests and rejoices in the fear of God.

~

Heavenly Father, as I grow — by Your grace and power — in living by Your practical and ethical wisdom, let my life bring You glory!

I rest and rejoice in recognizing Your supremacy over every area of my life and that You are the God who sends poverty and wealth, who humbles and exalts. "Wealth and honor come from you; you are the ruler of all things. In your hands are strength and power to exalt and give strength to all." 1 Chronicles 29:12

Thank You, Lord, for teaching us in Your Word that fearing You "is the beginning of wisdom." Psalm 111:10

With the angels in heaven, I praise You: "Amen! Praise and glory and wisdom and thanks and honor and power and strength be to our God for ever and ever. Amen!" Revelation 7:12

Day 25

WISE AND
JOYFUL LIVING

The principle that wisdom based on the fear of God ultimately leads to joyful living is taught over and over in the book of Proverbs, and throughout the Bible for that matter. One of its most meaningful illustrations for me is found in Proverbs 15:16-17: "Better a little with the fear of the LORD than great wealth with turmoil. Better a meal of vegetables where there is love than a fattened calf with hatred."

The particular principle set forth here is that love is more valuable than wealth. A "meal of vegetables" is descriptive of a poor-to-moderate living standard. In Solomon's day, ordinary people rarely had meat. On the other hand, "a fattened calf" connotes a wealthy family. With this background we can understand Solomon as saying that it's better to live in a poor family with love than in a wealthy family with hatred. This kind of wisdom can come only from the Lord.

The truth that love is more valuable than wealth ought to be self-evident. Yet throughout history, and especially in our culture today, it's obvious that wealth is deemed more valuable than love. People might deny that, but their actions speak louder than their words. Our society literally chases after wealth and possessions. This is true in inner-city ghettos as well as in up-scale suburbs. All levels of our society base their supposed happiness on their ability to acquire the possessions they want.

This drive to acquire money and possessions has wide-ranging social implications. To name one, many parents place their professions or jobs above their children. It often results in a "swinging door" syndrome at home whereby families seldom sit down together to a meal, let alone spend extended time together. Parents become alienated from each other, and children from their parents, all in the interest of acquiring more possessions.

Families who base their wisdom for living on the fear of God, however, recognize that "a man's life does not consist in the abundance of his possessions" (Luke 12:15). They esteem love far more than material things. Some of these families may indeed be blessed by God with wealth, but that isn't the defining characteristic of their lives.

The priority of love over possessions was brought home to me deeply and poignantly a number of years ago. My wife of twenty-five years was dying of cancer. We had been on the staff of a Christian organization all our married lives, and our income had usually hovered around barely adequate. If we went out to eat, it was to Burger King or the local cafeteria. We seldom had discretionary income.

Two things we did have lots of, though, were love and fun. My wife had elected to be a full-time, stay-at-home mom. She spent hours with the children when they were small, and after they were in school, she never missed a game or scholastic event in which they participated. When I left for the office each morning, she always stood at the door to wave a loving good-bye. Our standard of living could have been described by Solomon's expression as "a meal of vegetables." But we had lots of love and we enjoyed life.

With this history of twenty-five years of love and the realization that my wife was probably dying, I came across Proverbs 15:16-17 one day in my Bible reading. As I read I wept for joy. I wrote in the margin of my Bible, "Thank You, Father, for a home with love."

My wife has been with the Lord now for several years, but still today "her children arise and call her blessed" (Proverbs 31:28). There is joy in fearing God and in the wisdom that comes from it.

~

Thank You, Father, for bringing so much love into my life.

Thank You above all for pouring out Your life into my heart by the Holy Spirit, whom You have given us. Romans 5:5

Thank You, gracious Father, for bringing light into my life. You are the God who said, "Let light shine out of darkness," and You caused Your light to "shine in our hearts to give us the light of the knowledge of the glory of God in the face of Christ." 2 Corinthians 4:6

Thank You, gracious Father, for bringing so much joy into my life. I love You and believe in You, and You have filled me "with an inexpressible and glorious joy." 1 Peter 1:8

With Your Son, Jesus, I say, "Father, glorify your name!" John 12:28

There is in God all that may draw forth both wonder and delight. . . . We glorify God, when we are God-admirers; admire his attributes, which are the glistering beams by which the divine nature shines forth; his promises which are the charter of free grace, and the spiritual cabinet where the pearl of price is hid; the noble effects of his power and wisdom in making the world, which is called "the work of his fingers" (Psalm 8:3). To glorify God is to have God-admiring thoughts; to esteem him most excellent, and search for diamonds in this rock only.

We glorify God by praising him. . . . The Hebrew word Bara, *"to create," and* Barak, *"to praise," are little different, because the end of creation is to praise God. . . . In prayer we act like men; in praise we act like angels.*

Who would put anything in balance with the Deity? Who would weigh a feather against a mountain of gold? God excels all other things more infinitely than the sun, the light of a candle.

— THOMAS WATSON,
"MAN'S CHIEF END" IN
A BODY OF DIVINITY

Part V

I Want to Glorify You, O God . . .

AND ENJOY YOU FOREVER

~

Thy bountiful care, what tongue can recite?
It breathes in the air, it shines in the light;
It streams from the hills; it descends to the plain,
And sweetly distills in the dew and the rain.
— ROBERT GRANT, 1833

Then praise we God the Father,
and praise we God the Son,
And God the Holy Spirit,
eternal Three in One
Till all the ransomed number
fall down before the throne,
And honour, power, and glory
ascribe to God alone.
— HORATIO NELSON, 1864

Day 26

ENJOYING HIS PROVISION

To be blessed by God is no small thing. Imagine enjoying the favor of the wealthiest person in the world. Yet all of his riches could not buy you good health if you had an incurable disease. Regardless of how wealthy or how powerful someone might be, there's always a boundary beyond which he or she cannot go. But God has no boundaries. With Him nothing is impossible (Luke 1:37). And out of His limitless riches, He blesses those who fear Him — a fear that is deeply intertwined with giving glory to God, so that the psalmist can say of the Lord,

*Surely his salvation is near those who **fear** him,*
   *that his **glory** may dwell in our land.*
   (Psalm 85:9)

As I've studied the fear of God in the Psalms, I've noticed how often blessing is promised to those who fear Him. We read in Psalm 112:1, "*Blessed* is the man who fears the LORD, who finds great delight in his commands," and again in Psalm 128:4, "Thus is the man *blessed* who fears the LORD." In fact, there are fifteen or so passages on this subject. There is blessing in the fear of the Lord.

Many of these passages have to do with enjoying His provision. In Psalm 34:3 we read this invitation from David to give God glory: "Glorify the LORD with me; let us exalt his name together." Then we read this in verses 9-10:

> *Fear the LORD, you his saints,*
>   *for **those who fear him lack nothing**.*
> *The lions may grow weak and hungry,*
>   *but **those who seek the LORD***
>   ***lack no good thing**.*

Psalm 111 likewise focuses first on glorifying God: "I will extol the LORD with all my heart. . . . Glorious and majestic are his deeds" (verses 1,3). Then we read, "*He provides food for those who fear him;* he remembers his covenant forever" (verse 5). God promises to provide for those who fear Him.

Examples of this provision are found

throughout Scripture. One of the most notable is God's provision for the widow at Zarephath (1 Kings 17:7-15). She was gathering a few sticks to cook one last meal for herself and her son to eat — and then die — when the prophet Elijah said to her, "Don't be afraid. Go home and do as you have said. But first make a small cake of bread for me from what you have and bring it to me, and then make something for yourself and your son."

This was a bold request to make. A family is down to its last meager meal, and God's servant tells them to feed him first. But Elijah knew God was going to work a miracle to provide for the widow and her son as well as himself.

This is exactly what happened. "She went away and did as Elijah had told her. So there was food every day for Elijah and for the woman and her family. For the jar of flour was not used up and the jug of oil did not run dry, in keeping with the word of the LORD spoken by Elijah" (17:15-16).

Jesus gave us insight into this incident when He spoke of it in Luke 4:25-26: "I assure you that there were many widows in Israel in Elijah's time, when the sky was shut for three and a half years and there was a severe famine throughout the land. Yet Elijah was not sent to any of them, but to a widow in Zarephath in the region of Sidon."

God sent Elijah to the widow's house not just to provide for him but also to provide for the widow and her son. God could have provided for Elijah in any number of ways. In fact, He had earlier done so through some ravens (1 Kings 17:2-6). God didn't need the widow, but the widow needed Him. God had determined to provide for her need, but He did this as she herself provided for Elijah.

Here was a tangible expression of the fear of God. The widow, even though a Gentile and outside of God's covenant nation at the time, through faith obeyed God. She believed God's promise and obeyed His command, both of which were given to her through God's servant.

Hebrews 11:8 tells us that "by faith Abraham . . . obeyed." Obedience — one of those fundamental characteristics of the person who fears God — often requires an act of faith on our part. In fact, faith can sometimes be described as "obeying God and trusting Him for the results." This is what the widow did, thereby demonstrating her fear of God, and what we can do as well.

Praise God from whom all blessings flow!
  Father, by Your grace and power
    let me grow in enjoying
Your provision for all my needs,
    and let it all be for Your glory.
You are the One who "satisfies the thirsty
  and fills the hungry with good things."
Psalm 107:9

You have "filled the hungry with good things." Luke 1:53

"Those who seek the LORD lack no good thing." Psalm 34:10

"You open your hand and satisfy the desires of every living thing." Psalm 145:16

Day 27

HOW GOD PROVIDES

What God did for the widow in Elijah's day (1 Kings 17:7-15; Luke 4:25-26), He continues to do today for those who fear Him. It may not be a miraculous provision, but He does order His providences in such a way that He cares for those who fear Him.

Early in my experience in Christian ministry I needed a topcoat, having moved from a mild climate to a cold one. I priced a coat in a store but had no money to buy it. One day in the mail I received two letters. One contained a check from a friend for the exact amount of the price of the coat; the other had a request from a mission organization for funds. As I prayed over the funds request, I felt prompted to send the entire amount of the check I'd received to the mission. A few days later I received a second check in the mail, again for the price of the coat.

God intended to provide the coat I needed, but He also wanted to teach me to trust Him.

God's promise of provision to those who fear Him does raise a question, however. Does He always provide? Aren't there many instances of Christians starving, particularly in parts of Africa and Asia today? I've sometimes struggled with this question myself.

As we seek answers we must keep in mind that we'll never fully understand the ways of God in a specific situation. As Paul wrote, "How unsearchable His decisions, and how mysterious His methods!" (Romans 11:33, *Williams*).

We also need to realize that in God's manner of operating today, He most often supplies the needs of His people who are in dire straits through others who belong to Him. In fact, 2 Corinthians 8–9, the scriptures most often used to teach principles of Christian giving, were written specifically to address this issue: Christians who had plenty meeting the needs of those who had little. Rather than questioning God's faithfulness to His promises, we might better question our own faithfulness as stewards of the resources He has given to us.

You, O Lord, are my Shepherd, and I shall never be in want. "Surely goodness and love will follow me all the days of my life, and I will dwell in the house of the LORD forever." Psalm 23:1,6

"O LORD God Almighty, who is like you? You are mighty, O LORD, and your faithfulness surrounds you." Psalm 89:8

"Your love, O LORD, reaches to the heavens, your faithfulness to the skies." "Your faithfulness continues through all generations." Psalms 36:5; 119:90

"I will sing of the LORD's great love forever; with my mouth I will make your faithfulness known through all generations. I will declare that your love stands firm forever, that you established your faithfulness in heaven itself." Psalm 89:1-2

I will believe and testify of the truth of Your faithfulness. I will say, "The word of the LORD is right and true; he is faithful in all he does." Psalm 33:4

Day 28

ENJOYING HIS PROTECTION

A God-fearing person looks to God for protection from harm and danger. Psalm 33:16-18 says,

> *No king is saved by the size of his army;*
> *no warrior escapes by his great strength.*
> *A horse is a vain hope for deliverance;*
> *despite all its great strength it cannot save.*
> *But the eyes of the LORD*
> *are on those who fear him,*
> *on those whose hope is in his unfailing love.*

The contrast here is not between the *use* of human means and reliance upon God, but between *reliance* on human means and on God. The human means in the psalm are all taken from a military setting: the size of an army, the warrior's strength, and the strength of the cavalry horse. David, the author of this psalm, was a warrior himself, so he appreciated the importance of these human means, and he used them. Yet he turned his hope to God.

I try to be careful when I drive. Yet I know that however careful I may be, only God can protect me from a foolish mistake of my own or another driver. In the fear of God I must look to Him for protection.

The word-picture "eyes of the LORD" in Psalm 33 refers to His constant watch-care. A contemporary illustration would be the lifeguard at a swimming pool who constantly watches for signs of someone in trouble. But this illustration doesn't do justice to God's watch-care. The lifeguard might be distracted or looking toward the other end of the pool. He or she cannot watch every swimmer every moment. But God's eyes are never distracted, never turned away from us. In His infiniteness He carefully watches over each of His own every moment of their lives.

An additional promise of protection is in Psalm 145, another of David's songs. We observe once more a focus on glorifying God, followed by a promise to those who fear Him.

First, the view to His glory:

All you have made will praise you, O LORD;
your saints will extol you.
They will tell of the glory of your kingdom and
speak of your might,
so that all men may know of your mighty acts
and the glorious splendor of your kingdom.
(verses 10-12)

Then this promise in verse 19: "He fulfills the desires of those who fear him; he hears their cry and saves them." God not only watches over us; He listens for our cries for help and saves us. He's like a mother whose ears seem tuned to hear her baby's cry. He even sends His angel to encamp around those who fear Him (Psalm 34:7). None of us knows how many times an angel of God has protected us when we were not even aware of it.

But the question arises: Does God always save us from harm? Obviously the answer is no. How then do we resolve God's promise with the realities of life? We must see God's hand working to bring about His purposes for us, purposes that we often don't understand.

Trusting God in times of adversity is certainly one of the marks of a God-fearing person. And our trust will be rewarded — if not in this life, certainly in the life to come.

As William S. Plumer, a nineteenth-century theologian, wrote, "Among all the redeemed in glory there is not one who looks back and sees that on earth there was any mistake in the divine conduct towards him. God does all things well."[25]

∾

Mighty God, "You give me your shield of victory, and your right hand sustains me; you stoop down to make me great." Psalm 18:35

"O my Strength, I sing praise to you; you, O God, are my fortress, my loving God." Psalm 59:17

"For those who fear you, you have raised a banner to be unfurled against the bow." Psalm 60:4

My heart exclaims, "The LORD lives! Praise be to my Rock! Exalted be God my Savior!" "The glory of the LORD is great." Psalms 18:46; 138:5

You are "always before me" and "at my right hand," and for that reason, "I will not be shaken. Therefore my heart is glad and my tongue rejoices." Psalm 16:8-9

Day 29

ENJOYING HIS GUIDANCE

Psalm 25:12 states, "Who, then, is the man that fears the LORD? He will instruct him in the way chosen for him."

This instruction "in the way chosen for him" refers to the Lord's guidance in our lives. Christians often talk about "finding" or "knowing" the will of God in regard to a particular decision they must make. The thrust of Scripture, however, is not on our finding God's will but upon His guiding us. Psalm 23:3, for example, says, "He guides me in paths of righteousness for his name's sake." This is not the place to get into *how* God guides. I just want to point out that guidance is one of the blessings promised to those who fear God.

Not that God's guidance is always easy to discern and follow. Sometimes it *seems* as if He leaves us on our own to determine the best choice or course of action. But in the end, often in ways that surprise us, God guides us in His path for our lives. As we saw earlier in Psalm 139:16, our days were written in His book before one of them came to be, and He will sovereignly fulfill that plan in His own way. As I look back over a half-century of being a Christian, I can't think of a single instance where God failed to guide me in some important decision I needed to make.

Though it often seems as if God is not fulfilling His promises of provision or protection or guidance, yet we know God cannot lie or be untrue to His Word. As He said to Jeremiah, "I am watching over My word to perform it" (Jeremiah 1:12, NASB).

As those who seek to fear Him we may *plead* these promises before God, but we have to leave it to Him to fulfill them in the way and time He sees best for us. I emphasize the word *plead* because I prefer that word to the expression "claim the promises of God." The word *claim* suggests an obligation on God's part, which, of course, there is not. *Plead* on the other hand, acknowledges our helplessness and dependence on God, and, at the same time, recognizes that we have no claim upon Him.

Thank You, Good Shepherd, for guiding me

in paths of righteousness for Your name's sake.
Psalm 23:3

"You guide me with your counsel, and after-ward you will take me into glory." "If I rise on the wings of the dawn, if I settle on the far side of the sea, even there your hand will guide me, your right hand will hold me fast." Psalms 73:24; 139:9-10

In my heart I echo what Your Word pro-claims: "This God is our God for ever and ever; he will be our guide even to the end." Psalm 48:14

"In your unfailing love you will lead the people you have redeemed. In your strength you will guide them to your holy dwelling." Exodus 15:13

"Since you are my rock and my fortress, for the sake of your name lead and guide me." "Send forth your light and your truth, let them guide me." Psalms 31:3; 43:3

Day 30

ENJOYING HIS COMPASSION

One of my favorite passages of Scripture is Psalm 103. This song of praise both begins and ends with the exclamation, "Praise the LORD, O my soul." The entire psalm is a tribute to God's goodness, but I want to direct your attention especially to verses 8-18, which magnify God's compassion.

> *The LORD is compassionate and gracious,*
> *   slow to anger, abounding in love.*
> *He will not always accuse,*
> *   nor will he harbor his anger forever;*
> *he does not treat us as our sins deserve*
> *   or repay us according to our iniquities.*
> *For as high as the heavens are above the earth,*
> *   so great is his love for those who fear him;*
> *as far as the east is from the west,*
> *   so far has he removed our transgressions*
> *   from us.*
> *As a father has compassion on his children,*

so the LORD has compassion on those
    who fear him;
for he knows how we are formed,
    he remembers that we are dust.
As for man, his days are like grass,
    he flourishes like a flower of the field;
the wind blows over it and it is gone,
    and its place remembers it no more.
But from everlasting to everlasting
    the LORD's love is with those who fear him,
    and his righteousness with their
        children's children —
with those who keep his covenant
    and remember to obey his precepts.

Note that three times (verses 11,13,17) the psalmist refers to God's love or compassion to those who fear Him. And note the superlatives he uses. God's love is "as high as the heavens are above the earth" (verse 11) . He removes our transgressions from us "as far as the east is from the west" (verse 12). And His love is "from everlasting to everlasting" (verse 17). All three expressions suggest infinity. God's love and compassion are infinite toward those who fear Him.

Today the word *compassion* is used for pity or for the desire to relieve someone's distress. In Psalm 103, however, it refers to God's patience and forgiveness. He is "compassionate and gracious, slow to anger, abounding in love" (verse 8). "He does not treat us as our sins deserve or repay us according to our iniquities" (verse 10).

The overall message of this portion of Psalm 103 can be summed up in the words of verse 3: It is God "who forgives all your sins." This is the promise to those who fear Him. *He forgives all our sins.* Perhaps this is why Psalm 103 is one of my favorites. The longer I live, the more I see the sinful corruption of my heart, yet the more I see of God's love and compassion toward me. I'm glad the fear of the Lord has more to do with God's character than with mine.

We must never forget, though, why God so freely and completely forgives us. It's only because the penalty for our sins has already been borne by Christ. But the fact that Christ *has* paid our penalty should give us the assurance that God has indeed removed our sins from us as far as the east is from the west. We must always seek our assurance of forgiveness not only in God's compassion toward us but also in Christ's death for us.

So we see the promises of God's blessing to those who fear Him: His provision, protection, guidance, and compassion. Though these blessings are promised to those who fear God, they do not come to us *because* we fear God. They come to us because of the merit of Christ. He is the One who fully delighted in the fear of the Lord (Isaiah 11:3), and only He has ever perfectly feared God. Our fear of the Lord is always imperfect and inadequate. It could never, on its own merit, earn one iota of the blessings God has promised to those who fear Him. It is only "in Christ" that God's promises to those who fear Him are always "Yes" (2 Corinthians 1:20). Thus it is that God is glorified — just as we see in Paul's next words in this verse from 2 Corinthians: "And so through him the 'Amen' is spoken by us *to the glory of God.*"

So we do not fear God in order to earn His promised blessings. We fear Him because of who He is and what He has done for us. And then, out of the riches of His own grace in Christ, He fulfills His promises to those who fear Him, and thus He is glorified.

〜

"The earth is filled with your love, O LORD." "The LORD is good to all; he has compassion on all he has made." Your "compassions never fail. They are new every morning, great is your faithfulness." Psalms

119:64; 145:9; Lamentations 3:22-23

"I will exalt you, O LORD, for you lifted me out of the depths." "You are God my Savior, and my hope is in you all day long." Psalms 30:1; 25:5

Thank You for Your promise to all Your children, that if we confess our sins, You are "faithful and just and will forgive us our sins and purify us from all unrighteousness." 1 John 1:9

I worship, and praise You as "the Father of compassion and the God of all comfort." You are "close to the brokenhearted," and You offer salvation to "those who are crushed in spirit." "Your compassion is great, O LORD." 2 Corinthians 1:3; Psalms 34:18; 119:156

"To you, O LORD, I lift up my soul. You are forgiving and good, O LORD, abounding in love to all who call to you." Psalm 86:4-5

Day 31

A SCROLL OF REMEMBRANCE

We read in Malachi 3:16,

Then those who feared the LORD talked with each other, and the LORD listened and heard. A scroll of remembrance was written in his presence concerning those who feared the LORD and honored his name.

This passage was written in a time of deep spiritual decline among the Jews. They questioned God's love (1:2). They showed contempt for Him (1:6-7). They robbed God of the tithes and offerings due Him (3:8). And they said, "It is futile to serve God" (3:14).

In the midst of this national ungodliness, however, there was a group who feared and honored the Lord, and who talked to one another. Undoubtedly they encouraged one another in the same way Hebrews 3:13

teaches: "Encourage one another daily, as long as it is called Today, so that none of you may be hardened by sin's deceitfulness."

In commenting on Malachi 3:16, Matthew Henry wrote,

> *They spoke often one to another concerning the God they feared, and that name of his which they thought so much of; for out of the abundance of the heart the mouth will speak, and a good man, out of a good treasure there, will bring forth good things. Those that feared the Lord kept together as those that were company for each other; they spoke kindly and endearingly one to another, for the preserving and promoting of mutual love. . . . They spoke intelligently and edifyingly to one another, for the increasing and improving of faith and holiness.* [26]

And as these faithful, God-fearing, God-honoring people encouraged one another with their words, "the LORD listened and heard." This, of course, is a metaphorical expression, for God knows our words before they're even on our tongues. The expression is intended to convey that God took special notice of their words to one another.

After God listened, He had a scroll of remembrance written before Him concerning these people who feared Him and honored His name. God does not need a book of remembrance; being omniscient, He never forgets. Rather the scroll is an allusion to the "custom of ancient Near Eastern kings to have a record written of the most important events at their court and in their kingdom."[27] (See Esther 6:1-2 for a good example of this practice.) The "scroll of remembrance" in Malachi was God's way of giving special honor to those who feared and honored Him and who encouraged one another to do the same.

We live in a day much like the days of Malachi. Not only has society as a whole become ungodly, but even much of the church of Jesus Christ has failed to fear and glorify God. God is looked upon not as the One to be feared and honored, but as someone to meet our felt needs and help us with our problems. The church today is too much like the Jews of Isaiah's time, of whom he wrote,

> *They say to the seers,*
>   *"See no more visions!"*
> *and to the prophets,*
>   *"Give us no more visions of what is right!*
> *Tell us pleasant things,*
>   *prophesy illusions.*

Leave this way,
*   get off this path,*
* and stop confronting us*
*   with the Holy One of Israel!"*
*   (Isaiah 30:10-11)*

This is a description of so much of the Christianity we see around us today. "Tell us pleasant things, but above all, stop confronting us with the Holy One of Israel. Don't speak to us of fearing Him or honoring Him."

God does have His faithful ones, however. Even in these difficult days there are those who delight to fear and glorify God and who encourage others to do the same.

Are you one of those? If so, I pray that you and I will continue to grow in this delight until one day we hear those words of ultimate joy expressed in Matthew 25:23:

Well done, good and faithful servant! You have been faithful with a few things; I will put you in charge of many things.
*   Come and share your master's happiness!*

༄

Loving Father, remember me and deal with me according to Your goodness and compassion, according to the sacrifice and worth of Your Son, Jesus Christ. "Remember, O LORD, your great mercy and love, for they are from of old. Remember not the sins of my youth and my rebellious ways; according to your love remember me, for you are good, O LORD." Psalm 25:6-7

"You understand O LORD; remember me and care for me." Jeremiah 15:15

"In wrath remember mercy." Habakkuk 3:2

"Remember me, O LORD, when you show favor to your people." "Remember me with favor, O my God." Psalm 106:4; Nehemiah 13:31

"Jesus, remember me when you come into your kingdom." Luke 23:42

"Praise be to the LORD, for he has heard my cry for mercy.... My heart trusts in him, and I am helped. My heart leaps for joy and I will give thanks to him in song." Psalm 28:6-7

"O LORD my God, I will give you thanks forever." Psalm 30:12

"I will praise your name, O LORD, for it is good." Psalm 54:6

"Like your name, O God, your praise reaches to the ends of the earth." Psalm 48:10

"Praise the LORD. Praise the LORD, O my soul. I will praise the LORD all my life; I will *sing praise to my God as long as I live."* Psalm 146:1-2

Glory be to the Father, and to the Son, and to the Holy Spirit, as it was in the beginning, is now, and ever shall be, world without end. Amen.

It will be a great comfort in a dying hour, to think we have glorified God in our lives. It was Christ's comfort before his death: "I have glorified thee on the earth" (John 17:4, KJV). At the hour of death, all your earthly comforts will vanish: if you think how rich you have been, what pleasures you have had on earth; this will be so far from comforting you, that it will torment you the more. . . . But to have conscience telling you, that you have glorified God on the earth, what sweet comfort and peace will this let into your soul! How will it make you long for death!

How diligent and zealous should we be in glorifying God, that we may come at last to enjoy him! . . . If anything can make us rise off our bed of sloth, and serve God with all our might, it should be this, the hope of our near enjoyment of God for ever.

It is the enjoyment of God that makes heaven. . . . There shall be a loving of God, an acquiescence in him, a tasting his sweetness; not only inspection but possession. . . . We shall be continually in his presence, continually under divine raptures of joy. There shall not be one minute in heaven, wherein a glorified soul may say, I do not enjoy happiness.

— THOMAS WATSON,
"MAN'S CHIEF END" IN
A BODY OF DIVINITY

NOTES

1. John Piper, *Desiring God* (Portland, Oreg.: Multnomah, 1986), 73.
2. Sometimes the *New International Version* uses the word praise instead of *glorify*. When this occurs I have quoted from the *New American Standard Bible* to keep the word *glorify as* consistent usage.
3. R. C. H. Lenski, *The Interpretation of St. Paul's First and Second Epistles to the Corinthians* (Minneapolis: Augsburg, 1963), 425.
4. Simon J. Kistemaker, *New Testament Commentary, Exposition of the First Epistle to the Corinthians* (Grand Rapids: Baker, 1993), 358.
5. Matthew Henry, *A Commentary on the Whole Bible*, vol.6 (Old Tappan, N.J.: Revell, n.d.), 559.
6. Charles Hodge, *An Exposition of the*

First Epistle to the Corinthians (London: Banner of Truth Trust, 1959), 202-3.

7. Jerry Bridges, *Trusting God* (Colorado Springs: NavPress, 1988), 17.

8. E. F. Hallock, *Preacher Hallock* (Los Angeles: Acton House, 1976), 101.

9. D. A. Carson gives a helpful discussion of this tradition in D. A. Carson, *The Gospel According to John* (Grand Rapids: Eerdmans, 1991), 679-80.

10. Sinclair Ferguson, *Grow in Grace* (Colorado Springs: NavPress, 1984), 36.

11. John Murray, *Principles of Conduct* (Grand Rapids: Eerdmans, 1957), 236-7.

12. John Murray, *Principles of Conduct*, 233.

13. John Calvin, *New Testament Commentaries, The Epistles of Paul to the Romans and Thessalonians*, vol. 8 (Grand Rapids: Eerdmans, 1980), 67.

14. John Murray, *Principles of Conduct*, 229.

15. John Murray, *Principles of Conduct*, 236-7.

16. The *New International Version* sometimes uses the word *reverence* where most other translations have the phrase "fear of God." Examples of such usage are 2 Corinthians 7:1 and Colossians 3:22. My count of more than 150 includes instances where the NIV uses

reverence. Both the Hebrew word *yare* and the Greek word *phobos* carry the full range of meaning of *fear*, from dread or terror to reverence and awe. Both words are sometimes rendered as *reverence* by the NIV translators.

17. John Murray, *Principles of Conduct*, 231.

18. Rudolph Otto, *The Idea of the Holy* (New York: Oxford University Press, 1958), 10.

19. The title "Lord" with which Peter addressed Jesus is used again and again as an equivalent of God in the Septuagint, the Greek translation of the Old Testament that Peter would have known. See William Hendriksen's *New Testament Commentary, Exposition of the Gospel According to Luke* (Grand Rapids: Baker, 1978), 284.

20. John Calvin, *Institutes of the Christian Religion, The Knowledge of God the Creator*, bk. 1, ed. John T. McNeill, trans. Ford Lewis Battles (Philadelphia: Westminster, 1960), 38-9.

21. Sinclair Ferguson, *Grow in Grace*, 35.

22. John Bunyan, "A Treatise on the Fear of God," *The Works of John Bunyan*, vol. 1 (1875, reprint, Grand Rapids: Baker, 1977), 483. I have tried to capture the essence of Bunyan's statements rather

than quoting him, so as to make his thoughts more understandable for today's readers.

23. Sinclair Ferguson, *Grow in Grace*, 36.
24. Michael Denton, *Evolution: A Theory in Crisis* (Bethesda, Md.: Adler & Adler, 1985), 358-9.
25. William S. Plumer, *Psalms* (1867; reprint, Carlisle, Pa.: Banner of Truth, 1975), 419.
26. Matthew Henry, *A Commentary on the Whole Bible*, vol. 4, 1499.
27. Pieter A. Verhoef, *The Books of Haggai and Malachi, The New International Commentary on the Old Testament* (Grand Rapids: Eerdmans, 1987), 321.

SCRIPTURE INDEX

The employees of Thorndike Press hope you have enjoyed this Large Print book. All our Thorndike and Wheeler Large Print titles are designed for easy reading, and all our books are made to last. Other Thorndike Press Large Print books are available at your library, through selected bookstores, or directly from us.

For information about titles, please call:

(800) 223-1244

or visit our Web site at:

www.gale.com/thorndike
www.gale.com/wheeler

To share your comments, please write:

Publisher
Thorndike Press
295 Kennedy Memorial Drive
Waterville, ME 04901